MEATLESS DISHES FOR A CHANGE . . . OR A LIFETIME.

101 VEGETARIAN RECIPES

◆ Many Bean Salad with Sherry Marinade
◆ Artichoke and Leek Pie
◆ Red Pepper Risotto with Fresh Corn
◆ Linguine with Cauliflower and Toasted Bread Crumbs
◆ Mushrooms and Shallot Sauce
◆ Strawberry-Apple Tart

FRESH AND DELICIOUS DISHES FOR EASY
EVERYDAY MEALS
OR ABSOLUTELY ELEGANT DINING

101
VEGETARIAN
RECIPES

THE CORINNE T. NETZER GOOD EATING SERIES

▶▶▶▶▶▶▶▶▶▶▶▶▶

101 VEGETARIAN RECIPES

◆◆◆◆◆

Corinne T. Netzer

A Dell Trade Paperback

A DELL TRADE PAPERBACK

Published by
Dell Publishing
a division of
Bantam Doubleday Dell Publishing Group, Inc.
1540 Broadway
New York, New York 10036

Library of Congress Cataloging in Publication Data
Netzer, Corinne T.
101 vegetarian recipes / Corinne T. Netzer.
p.   cm.—(The Corinne T. Netzer good eating series)
Includes index.
ISBN 0-440-50597-6
1. Vegetarian cookery. I. Title. II. Title: One hundred one
vegetarian recipes. III. Series: Netzer, Corinne T. Good eating
series.
TX837.N46   1994
641.5'636—dc20   93-46366 CIP

Book designed by Rhea Braunstein

Illustrated by Alice Sorensen

Printed in the United States of America
Published simultaneously in Canada
September 1994
10 9 8 7 6 5 4 3 2 1
HCR

CONTENTS

INTRODUCTION

When it comes to food, no matter how good something is for you, you won't eat it unless it tastes good. *101 Vegetarian Recipes* brings you all the benefits of meatless meals plus all the contemporary tastes you want.

These recipes use a variety of ingredients, readily available in your supermarket, so whether you follow a vegetarian lifestyle or just want to decrease your meat intake without the continued boredom of nothing but steamed vegetables, this book provides you with recipes you can use to create gourmet meals on an everyday basis.

Each recipe lists a nutritional analysis based on the latest data supplied by the United States Department of Agriculture and various food producers and processors. Analysis is as accurate as possible; however, since counts may vary because of incalculable differences (i.e., sizes, moisture content, regional and seasonal variations in food) I must call it an approximate analysis.

To facilitate usage by those of you who are vegan, I have used the letter V after the serving size to indicate those recipes that have no lacto-/ovo-derived products among the ingredients.

I hope you enjoy the dishes in this book as much as I do.

C.T.N.

SAUCES, DRESSINGS, and CONDIMENTS

◆ ◆ ◆ ◆ ◆

MUSHROOM AND
SHALLOT SAUCE

▶ ▶

Serve this sauce over hot mashed potatoes, turnips, polenta, or broad noodles.

1   *ounce dried wild mushrooms (oyster, porcini,
     Chanterelle, etc.)*
     Boiling water
2   *teaspoons olive oil*
2   *large shallots, finely minced*
⅓   *cup dry white wine*
1   *cup water*
½   *teaspoon dried parsley*
½   *teaspoon dried thyme*
     Salt and freshly ground pepper to taste
1   *tablespoon fine flour*
¼   *cup soy milk or low fat milk*

1. Put mushrooms in a mixing bowl, add enough boiling water to cover and set aside to soften.

2. Heat oil in a nonstick skillet. Add shallots and stir over medium heat for about 5 minutes or until very lightly browned.

3. Drain mushrooms, reserving ¼ cup liquid. Mince mushrooms, add to skillet with shallots, and stir over medium-low heat for about 10 minutes or until shallots are well browned but not burned.

4. Add reserved mushroom liquid and wine to skillet, raise heat and bring to a boil. Reduce heat to medium, stir in

water, parsley, thyme, and season to taste with salt and pepper. Simmer for 20 minutes, stirring occasionally.

5. Dissolve flour in milk and stir into mushrooms in skillet. Stir until mixture is thickened and well blended. Taste and adjust seasonings, if necessary.

MAKES ABOUT 1¾ CUPS V

PER ¼ CUP SERVING: 45 CALORIES; 1.5 GRAMS PROTEIN; 5.5 GRAMS CARBOHYDRATES; 1.4 GRAMS FAT; 0 MILLIGRAMS CHOLESTEROL; 18 MILLIGRAMS SODIUM (WITHOUT SALTING).

◆ ◆ ◆ ◆ ◆

CHUNKY
SUN-DRIED TOMATO SAUCE

▶ ▶

Because all of the vegetables are coarsely chopped, this thick, full-flavored tomato sauce makes a hearty topping for your favorite pasta, rice, or unadorned vegetable dishes. Terrific spooned on crusty bread, over omelets, added to soups and stews . . . you name it! I treasure it as my perennial favorite all-purpose any-excuse-to-use-it sauce.

¾ cup sun-dried tomatoes (*not oil-packed*)
1 cup boiling water
2 teaspoons olive oil
1 large onion, coarsely chopped
1 stalk celery, coarsely chopped
1 small red or green bell pepper, trimmed and coarsely chopped
1 clove garlic, chopped
1 cup canned no-salt-added tomato sauce
½ cup dry red wine
½ teaspoon each: dried thyme, marjoram, rosemary, basil
1 teaspoon dried oregano
1 tablespoon chopped fresh Italian parsley
Salt and freshly ground pepper to taste

1. Cover sun-dried tomatoes with boiling water and let stand at least 10 minutes to soften. Drain, reserving water, and cut tomatoes into ½-inch pieces.
2. Heat oil in a large saucepan. Add onion, celery, and

bell pepper and stir over medium-low heat for about 10 minutes, or until vegetables are tender but not browned.

3. Add remaining ingredients, including sun-dried tomatoes and its water, and stir to blend. Reduce heat to low, cover, and simmer very gently for 30 minutes, stirring occasionally.

4. Uncover, raise heat to high and bring sauce to a low boil. Let boil, stirring, for 2 to 3 minutes or until slightly reduced. Remove from heat, taste and adjust seasonings, if necessary.

MAKES ABOUT 2 CUPS V
PER ¼ CUP SERVING: 50 CALORIES; 1.3 GRAMS PROTEIN; 9.0 GRAMS CARBOHYDRATES; 1.1 GRAMS FAT; 0 MILLIGRAMS CHOLESTEROL; 17 MILLIGRAMS SODIUM (WITHOUT SALTING).

◆ ◆ ◆ ◆ ◆

SPICY STIR-FRY
SAUCE

▶ ▶

Make your next stir-fried vegetables, noodles, or rice feel at home with this zingy, Oriental-inspired sauce.

To thicken sauce, stir in one tablespoon of cornstarch dissolved in three tablespoons of cold water and add to the mixture after it has been cooked.

½ *tablespoon chili oil or hot sesame oil*
2 *cloves garlic, finely chopped*
1 *tablespoon freshly grated ginger*
1 *cup sake (rice wine)*
¾ *cup Vegetable Stock (page 19) or canned low sodium broth*
1 *tablespoon low sodium soy sauce*

1. Heat oil in a medium saucepan and sauté garlic over medium heat until softened and very pale golden. Add ginger and stir to blend.

2. Raise heat and pour in remaining ingredients. Bring mixture to a boil, reduce heat and simmer for 10 minutes or until slightly reduced.

MAKES ABOUT 1¼ CUP V
PER ¼ CUP SERVING: 25 CALORIES; .5 GRAMS PROTEIN; 2.0 GRAMS CARBOHYDRATES; 1.5 GRAMS FAT; 0 MILLIGRAMS CHOLESTEROL; 135 MILLIGRAMS SODIUM (WITHOUT SALTING).

◆◆◆◆◆

TOMATO-HERB DRESSING

▶▶▶▶▶▶▶▶▶▶▶▶▶▶▶▶▶▶▶▶▶▶▶

Here's a delightfully different dressing for your next salad. Or, just heat and serve over steamed vegetables. It's also terrific mixed with rice, barley, orzo, or any of your other favorite grains.

1 *cup low sodium tomato juice*
2 *tablespoons red wine vinegar*
½ *tablespoon olive oil*
1 *small garlic clove, pressed*
¼ *teaspoon each: dried thyme, rosemary, and marjoram*
1 *teaspoon minced fresh parsley or ½ teaspoon dried*
Salt and freshly ground pepper to taste

Combine all ingredients in a jar with a tight-fitting lid. Cover well and shake until all ingredients are thoroughly blended.

MAKES ABOUT 1 CUP V

PER 1 TABLESPOON SERVING: 7 CALORIES; .2 GRAMS PROTEIN; .7 GRAMS CARBOHYDRATES; .4 GRAMS FAT; 0 MILLIGRAMS CHOLESTEROL; 2 MILLIGRAMS SODIUM (WITHOUT SALTING).

◆ ◆ ◆ ◆ ◆

FAT-FREE
VINAIGRETTE DRESSING

► ►

Vinaigrette is probably the most ubiquitous of all the dressings used for salads. In its most popular form, vinaigrette consists of oil, vinegar (usually three parts oil to one part vinegar), salt, and pepper. And since oil of any kind, be it olive or peanut, contains 14 grams of fat per tablespoon, the toll can be very hefty.

This version eliminates the oil completely. After experimenting with various ratios of water and lemon to vinegar, I found these proportions to be the most satisfying. As for the garlic, parsley, mustard, and tarragon . . . try them out first. You may wish to increase or decrease any combination of flavors and, by all means, have a go at it. But for an oil-less vinaigrette, I really think this one tastes very good.

    ½   cup red wine vinegar
    ½   cup water
        Juice from 1 large lemon
    2   small cloves garlic, pressed
    2   teaspoons minced fresh parsley or 1 teaspoon dried
    1   teaspoon dry mustard or to taste
    ½   teaspoon dried tarragon
        Salt and freshly ground pepper to taste

Combine all ingredients in a jar with a tight-fitting lid. Shake until all ingredients are thoroughly blended. Refrigerate and shake before using.

MAKES ABOUT 1¼ CUPS V

PER 1 TABLESPOON SERVING: 2 CALORIES; .1 GRAMS PROTEIN;
.4 GRAMS CARBOHYDRATES; 0 GRAMS FAT; 0 MILLIGRAMS
CHOLESTEROL; 2 MILLIGRAMS SODIUM (WITHOUT SALTING).

TANGY
TOMATO-GARLIC CATSUP

▶ ▶

The name "ketchup" is said to derive from *Ke-tsiap*—a spicy pickled-fish condiment popular in 17th-century China. Called "ketchup," "catchup," and more frequently, "catsup," this thick, spicy sauce usually starts with a tomato base along with vinegar to build its spunky character, while sugar, salt, and spices add balance to the blend.

In this version, garlic and dry mustard spike the brew, delivering a full-bodied taste. Use as a sassy alternative to bottled catsup.

> 1 *28-ounce can no-salt-added tomato purée*
> 2 *cloves garlic, minced*
> 2 *teaspoons sugar*
> 2 *teaspoons dry mustard*
> 2 *tablespoons red wine vinegar*
> *Salt and freshly ground pepper to taste*

Combine all ingredients and bring to a boil. Lower heat slightly and simmer, stirring often, for about 30 minutes or until mixture is reduced by half. Let cool before serving, or refrigerate for future use.

MAKES ABOUT 1 CUP V

PER 1 TABLESPOON SERVING: 25 CALORIES; .9 GRAMS PROTEIN; 5.5 GRAMS CARBOHYDRATES; .1 GRAM FAT; 0 MILLIGRAMS CHOLESTEROL; 10 MILLIGRAMS SODIUM (WITHOUT SALTING).

◆ ◆ ◆ ◆

RED PEPPER
AND CELERY RELISH

▶ ▶

Top your favorite pita fillers or sandwich stuffers with this addictive relish; or use it as an accompaniment to any bean or vegetable casserole.

> *Vegetable oil cooking spray*
> 2 *stalks celery, finely chopped*
> 1 *large red bell pepper, trimmed and finely chopped*
> 1 *medium red onion, chopped*
> 3 *tablespoons red wine vinegar*
> 1 *teaspoon sugar*
> *Salt and freshly ground pepper to taste*

1. Lightly coat a nonstick skillet with cooking spray. Add celery, pepper, and onion and cook, stirring, over low heat for 2 to 4 minutes or until vegetables start to soften; do not let vegetables brown.

2. Add remaining ingredients, reduce heat to low and simmer gently, stirring often, for an additional 5 minutes or until liquid is reduced and ingredients are thoroughly blended.

3. Remove from heat and let cool to room temperature before serving or refrigerate for future use.

MAKES ABOUT 2 CUPS V

PER 2 TABLESPOON SERVING: 6 CALORIES; .1 GRAMS PROTEIN; 1.4 GRAMS CARBOHYDRATES; .1 GRAM FAT; 0 MILLIGRAMS CHOLESTEROL; 5 MILLIGRAMS SODIUM (WITHOUT SALTING).

◆ ◆ ◆ ◆ ◆

GINGERED PEACH
AND PEPPER CHUTNEY

▶ ▶

Chutney, derived from the East Indian word *chatni*, is a spicy condiment consisting of fruit, vinegar, sugar, and spices. With a texture that can range from chunky to smooth and in degree of spiciness from mild to hot, chutney is usually served as an accompaniment to curried dishes.

Because of the sweet (peaches, peppers, currants, onion, brown sugar, and nutmeg), sour (vinegar), spicy (ginger, cayenne) blend of this mixture, the resultant chutney makes a heavenly spread.

> 3   *large just-ripe peaches, peeled, pitted, and cut into chunks*
> 1   *red or yellow bell pepper, trimmed and diced*
> 1   *medium red onion, diced*
> 1   *tablespoon dried currants*
> 1   *cup cider vinegar*
> 2   *tablespoons brown sugar*
> 2   *tablespoons freshly grated ginger root, or to taste*
> 1   *teaspoon nutmeg*
>   *Dash cayenne pepper (optional)*
>   *Salt and freshly ground pepper to taste*

1. Combine all ingredients in a large saucepan. Cover and simmer over low heat for 45 minutes, stirring often.

2. Uncover, raise heat to medium and continue to simmer until mixture cooks down. Let cool before serving or refrigerating.

MAKES ABOUT 2 CUPS V

PER 1 TABLESPOON SERVING: 10 CALORIES; .1 GRAMS PRO-
TEIN; 2.7 GRAMS CARBOHYDRATES; 0 GRAMS FAT; 0 MILLI-
GRAMS CHOLESTEROL; 2 MILLIGRAMS SODIUM (WITHOUT
SALTING).

◆◆◆◆◆
PLUM ALMOND CHUTNEY

▶▶▶▶▶▶▶▶▶▶▶▶▶▶▶▶▶▶▶▶▶▶▶

Fragrant, simultaneously hot, sweet, and sour, this dense blend of fruit, nuts, and spices is the perfect partner for all your curried dishes, waffles, pancakes, breads, and muffins. In fact, you'll want to invent excuses to use it!

3	*cups peeled, pitted plums*
2	*tablespoons coarsely chopped blanched almonds*
1	*small onion, chopped*
1	*clove garlic, minced*
¾	*cup white vinegar or fruit vinegar*
¼	*cup fresh orange juice*
	Zest of one orange
¼	*cup honey*
1	*teaspoon freshly grated ginger*
¼	*teaspoon nutmeg*
	Dash almond extract, or to taste
	Pinch cayenne pepper, or to taste

Combine all ingredients in a large saucepan and bring to a boil. Reduce heat and cook, uncovered, at a bare simmer for 1 hour, stirring occasionally. Stir in additional orange juice, by the tablespoonful, if mixture gets too thick.

MAKES ABOUT 2 CUPS V
PER 1 TABLESPOON SERVING: 12 CALORIES; .3 GRAMS PROTEIN; 4.0 GRAMS CARBOHYDRATES; .1 GRAMS FAT; 0 MILLIGRAMS CHOLESTEROL; 2 MILLIGRAMS SODIUM (WITHOUT SALTING).

◆ ◆ ◆ ◆ ◆

DRIED FRUIT SPREAD

▶ ▶

With its blend of stewed prunes and apricots, think of this recipe as spreadable compote. As a plus, the aroma of the fruits and flavorings combining during the cooking process will definitely appeal to you. It keeps well tightly covered in the refrigerator.

1	cup dried pitted prunes, rinsed
1½	cups dried apricots, rinsed
2	tablespoons sugar
½	teaspoon cinnamon
¼	teaspoon nutmeg
2	teaspoons fresh lemon juice

1. Combine prunes and apricots in a saucepan. Add enough water to just cover fruit. Bring to a boil, then reduce heat and simmer gently for 40 minutes, stirring occasionally. Drain fruit and reserve ½ cup of the cooking liquid. Let fruits and liquid cool slightly.

2. Purée fruits in food processor and return to saucepan. Add reserved cooking liquid and remaining ingredients. Boil for about 5 minutes, stirring constantly to prevent scorching. Let cool, then refrigerate.

MAKES ABOUT 2 CUPS V
PER 1 TABLESPOON SERVING: 35 CALORIES; .4 GRAMS PROTEIN; 9.0 GRAMS CARBOHYDRATES; 0 GRAMS FAT; 0 MILLIGRAMS CHOLESTEROL; 2 MILLIGRAMS SODIUM (WITHOUT SALTING).

STOCKS and SOUPS

◆ ◆ ◆ ◆

VEGETABLE STOCK

▶ ▶

This basic stock can be modified to suit your individual taste. For example, add fresh or canned chopped tomatoes with their juice for a rich tomato-y flavor and color, or add diced sweet potatoes, parsnips, turnips or other winter vegetables for a sweeter, deeper taste; fennel will give it a slight licorice bent, and a few discs of ginger root will lend its own zip to your stock. While it is not necessary to sauté the vegetables first, I find that doing so seems to amplify their flavors. Use the proportions outlined in this recipe, but, by all means, experiment with your own favorite combinations.

This stock can be refrigerated for up to three days or frozen for future use.

1   teaspoon vegetable oil
2   medium leeks, chopped, or 2 cups chopped onions
2   carrots, diced or sliced
2   large stalks celery, with tops, coarsely chopped
1   small clove garlic, coarsely chopped
2   fresh thyme sprigs or ½ teaspoon dried
8   cups water
1   bay leaf
6   sprigs fresh parsley
2   medium potatoes, unpeeled, quartered
6   whole peppercorns
    Salt to taste

1. Heat oil in a nonstick soup pot. Add leeks, carrots, and celery and stir over medium-low heat for 2 minutes or

until vegetables start to soften; do not let them brown. Add garlic and cook an additional minute.

2. Add remaining ingredients and bring to a boil. Reduce heat to low and cook at a bare simmer for 45 minutes or until mixture is fragrant and all vegetables are tender. Taste and adjust seasonings, if necessary.

3. Strain stock immediately, reserving vegetables for another use if desired. If not using stock immediately, let cool to room temperature before refrigerating or freezing.

MAKES ABOUT 6 CUPS V
PER 1 CUP SERVING: 25 CALORIES; .5 GRAMS PROTEIN; 5.0 GRAMS CARBOHYDRATES; .5 GRAMS FAT; 0 MILLIGRAMS CHOLESTEROL; 35 MILLIGRAMS SODIUM (WITHOUT SALTING).

◆ ◆ ◆ ◆

RICH MUSHROOM
AND HERB STOCK

▶ ▶

A complex and sophisticated blend of mushrooms and
vegetables make this an elegant coating for tiny pasta or
rice. Combine with vegetables, grains, or reduce it to
produce a flavorful sauce. Use whenever a full-flavored
stock is called for.

This stock may be refrigerated for up to three days or
frozen for future use.

2   *ounces dried wild mushrooms (oyster, porcini,*
     and/or Chanterelle, etc.)
1   *cup hot water*
½   *tablespoon olive oil*
1   *large yellow onion, coarsely chopped*
2   *large carrots, sliced*
2   *stalks celery, sliced*
2   *large cloves garlic, flattened*
1½   *teaspoons dried* herbes de Provence *or mixture*
     of rosemary, marjoram, thyme, sage
5   *ounces white mushrooms, cleaned, trimmed, and*
     sliced
1   *cup Burgundy or other fruity red wine*
8   *cups water*
1   *large bay leaf*
     Pinch cayenne pepper
2   *teaspoons low sodium soy sauce*
     Salt and freshly ground pepper to taste

1. Soak dried wild mushrooms in hot water for 45 minutes.

2. While mushrooms soften, heat oil in a large nonstick stockpot and sauté onion over low heat, stirring occasionally, for 10 minutes or until onion is very soft and beginning to brown. Add carrots, celery, garlic, and herbs and cook, stirring more frequently, until onions are deeply browned and vegetables are soft.

3. Add white mushrooms and cook until just heated, then add wine, water, bay leaf, cayenne, soy sauce, and salt and pepper.

4. Drain wild mushrooms, reserving liquid. Chop mushrooms and add with reserved liquid to pot. Bring mixture to a boil, lower heat to a bare simmer, and cook, uncovered, for 45 minutes or until stock is very fragrant. Taste and adjust seasonings, if necessary.

5. Strain stock immediately, reserving vegetables for another use if desired. If not using immediately let cool to room temperature before refrigerating or freezing.

MAKES ABOUT 6 CUPS V
PER 1 CUP SERVING: 20 CALORIES; .5 GRAMS PROTEIN; 3.5 GRAMS CARBOHYDRATES; .4 GRAMS FAT; 0 MILLIGRAMS CHOLESTEROL; 100 MILLIGRAMS SODIUM (WITHOUT SALTING).

◆ ◆ ◆ ◆

RED LENTIL
AND SPINACH SOUP

▶ ▶

Although not exactly a quick meal, this soup is really rather simple to prepare, and most of your time will be spent waiting for the lentils to become tender.

I find this soup attractive with the lovely pellets of lentils and ribbons of spinach floating about in the tomato-tinged soup. A mother lode of healthy ingredients, this hearty protein- and fiber-laden soup is like a flavorful vitamin pill to me.

Serve with multigrain bread and a light salad or plain white or brown rice cooked in my Vegetable Stock (page 19).

1	cup red lentils, rinsed and picked over
5	cups water
1	bay leaf
	Salt and freshly ground pepper to taste
2	teaspoons vegetable oil
1	medium onion, diced
1	clove garlic, minced
10	ounces fresh spinach, trimmed, rinsed, and shredded
1	cup canned no-salt-added tomato sauce
	Pinch cayenne pepper (optional)

1. Combine lentils, water, bay leaf, and salt and pepper in a large soup pot. Bring to a boil, then reduce heat to low and simmer gently, stirring occasionally, for about 40 minutes or until lentils are just tender.

2. While lentils cook, heat oil in a skillet. Add onion and garlic and stir over medium heat until golden. Stir in spinach, reduce heat, cover, and simmer gently for about 5 minutes, or until spinach is well wilted. Stir.

3. Add spinach and contents of skillet to lentils and stir in tomato sauce and cayenne, if desired. Continue to simmer for an additional 10 minutes. Before serving, remove bay leaf and adjust seasoning, if necessary.

SERVES 4 V

PER SERVING: 250 CALORIES; 16.2 GRAMS PROTEIN; 41.7 GRAMS CARBOHYDRATES; 2.1 GRAMS FAT; 0 MILLIGRAMS CHOLESTEROL; 65 MILLIGRAMS SODIUM (WITHOUT SALTING).

◆ ◆ ◆ ◆ ◆

CREAMY LEEK
AND BEAN SOUP

▶ ▶

Comforting and nutritious, this tasty soup is indeed creamy . . . *not* creamed! "Creamy" refers to its texture only, for there's no cream in its content. By processing the white beans with the delicious leeks/onions/celery-based stock until you have a chunky purée and then adding soy or low fat milk, you will produce a dreamy, creamy soup at once rich and yet subtle in flavor.

Serve with crusty French or Italian bread, flavored bread sticks, or feature with Quinoa Salad (page 78) and a small salad of greens.

½   *tablespoon olive oil*
2   *leeks, white and tender green parts, rinsed and chopped*
1   *onion, chopped*
1   *stalk celery, chopped*
4   *cups Vegetable Stock (page 19) or canned low sodium broth*
1½ *cups cooked white beans, or canned (low sodium or well rinsed)*
    Salt and freshly ground pepper to taste
1   *cup soy milk or low fat milk*
4   *teaspoons snipped chives or finely sliced scallion greens*

1. Heat oil in a nonstick soup pot. Add leeks, onion, and

celery. Stir over medium heat for 5 minutes. Reduce heat and simmer gently an additional 5 minutes.

2. Add stock, beans, and salt and pepper. Cover and simmer gently for 15 minutes. Remove from heat and let cool slightly.

3. Transfer soup to a food processor and process briefly, until beans are coarsely puréed (do this in several batches if necessary). Return soup to pot.

4. Add milk and stir over medium heat for 5 minutes, or until well blended and thoroughly heated.

5. Transfer to individual heated bowls, sprinkle center of each with a teaspoon of chives or scallions, and serve.

SERVES 4 V

PER SERVING: 200 CALORIES; 10.0 GRAMS PROTEIN; 29.7 GRAMS CARBOHYDRATES; 4.1 GRAMS FAT; 0 MILLIGRAMS CHOLESTEROL; 100 MILLIGRAMS SODIUM (WITHOUT SALTING).

◆◆◆◆◆

FENNEL AND WATERCRESS SOUP
WITH GARLIC CROUTONS

▶▶▶▶▶▶▶▶▶▶▶▶▶▶▶▶▶▶▶▶▶▶▶▶

There are two kinds of people in this world: those who love fennel and those who hate it. I belong to the former group of folks who like the licorice flavor. But I have found that even the fiercest fennel foes are won over by the sweet, clean, delicate taste it exudes when cooked. Rich in vitamin A, fennel contains a good amount of calcium, phosphorus, and potassium, and can be eaten raw in salads, or braised, sautéed, and used in soups.

Enjoy this aromatic and savory soup as an elegant light lunch or as an auspicious prelude to dinner.

2	teaspoons vegetable oil
2	medium fennel bulbs (about 1 pound), coarsely chopped
1	medium onion, chopped
1	clove garlic, chopped
6	cups Vegetable Stock (page 19), canned low sodium broth, or water
2	medium white potatoes, peeled and cubed
	Salt and freshly ground pepper to taste
½	bunch watercress, well rinsed and chopped
2	tablespoons chopped fresh parsley
⅓	cup evaporated low fat milk
	Watercress or parsley sprigs for garnish
2	slices whole wheat bread, toasted, rubbed with cut garlic, and cut into croutons

1. Heat oil in a large nonstick soup pot and sauté fennel and onion over low heat, stirring frequently, until vegetables are soft. Add garlic and cook 2 minutes. Do not let vegetables or garlic brown.

2. Add stock, potatoes, and salt and pepper. Bring mixture to a boil, reduce heat and simmer for 30 minutes or until fennel is very tender. Add watercress and parsley and simmer until wilted.

3. Remove pot from heat and purée half of mixture in a food processor. Return puréed mixture to pot, stir in milk and heat through. Do not boil. Serve in heated soup plates garnished with watercress or parsley sprigs and croutons.

SERVES 4

PER SERVING: 185 CALORIES; 6.1 GRAMS PROTEIN; 31.0 GRAMS CARBOHYDRATES; 3.8 GRAMS FAT; .2 MILLIGRAMS CHOLESTEROL; 286 MILLIGRAMS SODIUM (WITHOUT SALTING).

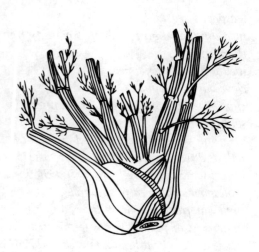

◆ ◆ ◆ ◆ ◆

HERBED
VEGETABLE SOUP

▶ ▶

Herbs are the fragrant leaves of plants that do not have woody stems and can be purchased in dried or fresh forms (whereas spices are pungent or aromatic offerings obtained from the bark, buds, fruit, roots, seeds, or stems of various plants and trees). Herbs, along with spices, condiments, vinegars and, of course, salt and pepper, are all known as "seasonings"; that is, ingredients that are added to food to intensify or improve its flavor.

The prudent addition of fresh parsley, plus dried thyme, rosemary, marjoram, and tarragon brings out the flavors of the vegetables and stock of this lovely and fragrant soup. Topped with a few gratings of fresh Parmesan or Romano cheese, it is excellent on its own as a midday reward or as the start of a dinnertime meal.

> 2 teaspoons olive oil
> 1 medium onion, chopped
> 1 clove garlic, chopped
> 2 medium carrots, diced
> 1 stalk celery, diced or sliced
> 6 cups Vegetable Stock (page 19), or canned low sodium broth, or water
> 1 large red potato, peeled and cubed
> 2 tablespoons chopped fresh parsley
> ½ teaspoon dried thyme
> ¼ teaspoon dried rosemary
> ⅛ teaspoon dried marjoram

Pinch dried tarragon
Salt and freshly ground pepper to taste

1. Heat oil in a large nonstick soup pot, and sauté onion and garlic over medium heat until onion is tender. Add carrots and celery and cook until onion shows flecks of gold.
2. Add stock and all remaining ingredients, except salt and pepper, and bring to a boil. Lower heat and simmer, covered, for 20 minutes or until potato and vegetables are very tender.
3. Mash ingredients lightly (do not purée), taste and add salt if desired, and several grindings of pepper.

SERVES 4 V

PER SERVING: 120 CALORIES; 2.4 GRAMS PROTEIN; 21.5 GRAMS CARBOHYDRATES; 3.2 GRAMS FAT; 0 MILLIGRAMS CHOLESTEROL; 125 MILLIGRAMS SODIUM (WITHOUT SALTING).

◆ ◆ ◆ ◆ ◆

CABBAGE, DILL,
AND BEAN SOUP

▶ ▶

I love the taste of cabbage! Moreover, cabbage is in the cruciferous vegetable family (of which Brussels sprouts, broccoli, cauliflower, and kale are members), is low in calories, rich in fiber and vitamin C and, like its relatives, has cancer-protecting potential.

Eastern Europeans have long enjoyed the happy marriage of cabbage, potatoes, and the green wisps of dill weed which I've combined here with beans for a soup that is both healthy and hearty.

2   cups shredded red cabbage
2   medium potatoes, peeled and diced
4   cups Vegetable Stock (page 19) or canned low
    sodium broth
1   medium onion, diced
1   cup chopped fresh dill weed
1   large fresh tomato, roughly chopped
1   cup cooked white beans, or canned (no-salt-added
    or well rinsed and drained)
    Salt and freshly ground pepper to taste
1   tablespoon minced fresh parsley

1. Combine cabbage, potatoes, stock, onion, dill, and tomato in a soup pot. Cover and bring to a simmer. Reduce heat to low and cook, stirring occasionally, for about 20 minutes or until potatoes are tender.

2. Stir beans into soup pot. Season to taste with salt and

pepper and continue simmering until all ingredients are heated through. Serve garnished with fresh parsley.

SERVES 4 V
PER SERVING: 158 CALORIES; 7.0 GRAMS PROTEIN; 31.7 GRAMS CARBOHYDRATES; .7 GRAMS FAT; 0 MILLIGRAMS CHOLESTEROL; 80 MILLIGRAMS SODIUM (WITHOUT SALTING).

◆ ◆ ◆ ◆ ◆

OLD-FASHIONED
TOMATO-RICE SOUP

▶ ▶

I have many fond memories of tomato-rice soup steeping on my mother's stove. It gave me a sense of well-being to sip or rather slurp it, much to my mother's chagrin. Whether your mom's soup came straight out of that familiar red and white can, or was created "from scratch," this recipe is sure to stir up emotions of comfort and joy.

It's terrific with garlic-rubbed rounds of toasted French bread, or as part of a soup 'n' sandwich lunch or light supper.

1	tablespoon olive oil
1	cup chopped white onion
2	cloves garlic, chopped
1½	pounds peeled fresh, ripe tomatoes or 28-ounce can no-salt-added plum tomatoes, juice reserved
¼	cup dry red wine
4	cups Vegetable Stock (page 19), canned low sodium broth, or water
½	teaspoon sugar (optional)
2	tablespoons chopped fresh basil or parsley
1	tablespoon chopped fresh thyme or 1 teaspoon dried
¾	cup uncooked long grain white rice
	Salt and freshly ground pepper to taste

1. Heat oil in a nonstick soup pot. Add onion and sauté over medium heat, stirring frequently, for 5 to 10 minutes or

until well softened. Add garlic and cook for an additional 2 minutes.

2. Raise heat to high and add tomatoes with its juice, and wine. Bring to a boil, stirring, and add stock. Return mixture to a boil, reduce heat and simmer gently for 30 minutes. If mixture becomes too thick, add additional stock or water by ¼ cupfuls. Taste and add sugar, if desired.

3. Stir in herbs and rice, cover and simmer for 20 minutes or until rice is tender. Taste, adjust seasonings and add salt and pepper, if desired.

SERVES 4 V

PER SERVING: 240 CALORIES; 5.4 GRAMS PROTEIN; 46.3 GRAMS CARBOHYDRATES; 4.3 GRAMS FAT; 0 MILLIGRAMS CHOLESTEROL; 105 MILLIGRAMS SODIUM (WITHOUT SALT-ING).

◆ ◆ ◆ ◆ ◆

ARTICHOKE SOUP

▶ ▶

Did you know that the globe artichoke is the bud of a large plant from the thistle family? Or that virtually all of the artichoke is edible . . . save for the nasty, prickly choke that serves to guard its prized heart? Also, artichokes are loaded with fiber, low in calories, and provide some potassium, vitamin A, calcium, iron, and protein. Fresh artichokes are available year round and keep well for several days in the refrigerator. Hearts of artichoke are available canned or frozen; artichoke bottoms are sold canned.

This soup showcases the delicate flavor of artichoke hearts that are first sautéed along with shallots and garlic, then boiled in a light, flavor-filled liquid of seasoned stock and milk—producing a fragrant pot of pale green velvet you'll find as lovely to look at as it is to eat.

1	tablespoon olive oil
2	cups sliced artichoke hearts, cooked, canned in unsalted water, or frozen and thawed
2	large shallots, minced
1	clove garlic, minced
3	cups Vegetable Stock (page 19) or water
1	bay leaf
1½	cups evaporated skim milk
1	teaspoon lemon juice
	Salt and white pepper to taste

1. Heat oil in a large soup pot. Add artichoke hearts and shallots and cook over medium heat, stirring frequently,

until vegetables are softened but not browned. Add garlic and cook for 1 minute.

2. Add stock or water and bay leaf, bring to a boil, reduce heat and simmer gently for 30 minutes or until artichokes are very tender. Remove and discard bay leaf.

3. Purée half of mixture in a food processor and return to pot. Stir briefly over low heat and add milk, lemon juice, and salt and pepper. Heat through but do not boil. Serve hot or chilled.

SERVES 4

PER SERVING: 180 CALORIES; 10.5 GRAMS PROTEIN; 26.4 GRAMS CARBOHYDRATES; 4.0 GRAMS FAT; 3.7 MILLIGRAMS CHOLESTEROL; 240 MILLIGRAMS SODIUM (WITHOUT SALTING).

◆ ◆ ◆ ◆ ◆

CARROT VICHYSSOISE

▶ ▶

This rich soup is classically made from potato and leek and cream. It is served both cold and hot, and is traditionally garnished with chopped chives. In this version, carrots, leeks, and potatoes are combined along with seasonings and skim milk. Top with a sprinkle of chopped scallion, snipped chives or dill, and serve with sesame bread sticks, melba toast, or matzo crackers.

2   teaspoons vegetable oil
2   large leeks, white bulb only, well rinsed and
     chopped
1   clove garlic, chopped
3   cups Vegetable Stock (page 19), or canned low
     sodium broth, or water
2   medium potatoes, peeled and cubed
2   medium carrots, cut into 1-inch slices
1   cup evaporated skim milk
     Salt and freshly ground pepper to taste
2   tablespoons finely minced scallions or chopped
     chives

1. Heat oil in a nonstick soup pot. Add leeks and garlic and cook, stirring frequently, over medium-low heat for about 8 minutes or until leeks are tender; do not let brown.

2. Add stock, potatoes, and carrots to pot. Cover, reduce heat to low and simmer very gently for about 30 minutes or until potatoes and carrots are very tender. Remove from heat and let soup cool slightly.

3. Transfer soup to a food processor and process until smoothly puréed, then return to soup pot.

4. Stir in milk and season to taste with salt and pepper. Cook over very low heat, stirring frequently, for about 5 minutes or until ingredients are hot and thoroughly blended. If soup is too thick, add a little water. Remove from heat and cool to room temperature. Cover and refrigerate until well chilled.

5. To serve, stir soup and transfer to individual chilled bowls; sprinkle top of each with ½ tablespoon scallions or chives.

SERVES 4

PER SERVING: 205 CALORIES; 7.5 GRAMS PROTEIN; 33.7 GRAMS CARBOHYDRATES; 3.1 GRAMS FAT; 2.5 MILLIGRAMS CHOLESTEROL; 155 MILLIGRAMS SODIUM (WITHOUT SALTING).

◆ ◆ ◆ ◆ ◆

CHILLED
FRESH TOMATO-BASIL SOUP

▶ ▶

In summers past, when the bounty from the garden or roadside stands was particularly abundant, tomatoes coupled with basil seemed to be *the* romance of the season. However, this is one pairing that need not break up at summer's end, because hothouse tomatoes from Israel and Holland are available throughout the year, as is basil from the kinder climes of the western states. Still, the tomato-basil union is most enjoyable in the summertime when just-picked tomatoes and basil are at their peak. And nothing brings out their unique fresh flavors more than this aromatic no-cook soup. Just a few whirs of the blender or processor and you've got one of the most refreshing tureens around.

Serve with toasted pita triangles or a crusty multigrain loaf of bread.

1	small onion, quartered
2	large cloves garlic, quartered
4	ripe large fresh tomatoes
1½	cups low sodium tomato juice
1	cup water
1	tablespoon balsamic vinegar
½	cup chopped fresh basil
	Dash hot pepper sauce (optional)
	Salt and freshly ground pepper to taste
2	tablespoons finely minced fresh basil

1. Put onion and garlic in a food processor and process for a few seconds.

2. Cut tomatoes into pieces and add, with its juice, to food processor. Process until tomatoes are coarsely puréed.

3. Add all remaining ingredients, except the 2 tablespoons minced basil, and process very briefly to blend. Transfer mixture to a large bowl, cover, and refrigerate until well chilled, stirring occasionally.

4. Spoon soup into chilled bowls, sprinkle each with ½ tablespoon minced basil and serve.

SERVES 4 V

PER SERVING: 55 CALORIES; 2.0 GRAMS PROTEIN; 12.0 GRAMS CARBOHYDRATES; .5 GRAMS FAT; 0 MILLIGRAMS CHOLESTEROL; 20 MILLIGRAMS SODIUM (WITHOUT SALTING).

APPETIZERS
and
STARTERS

◆◆◆◆◆

STUFFED ZUCCHINI

▶▶▶▶▶▶▶▶▶▶▶▶▶▶▶▶▶▶▶▶▶▶▶▶▶▶

These zucchini "boats" make a rather nice presentation for the start of any meal.

4   small zucchini, about 4 inches long
    Vegetable oil cooking spray
2   teaspoons olive oil
1   large shallot, minced
¼   cup diced water chestnuts
¼   cup minced fresh Italian parsley
3   tablespoons dry white wine
1   tablespoon flour
    Fine bread crumbs, made from 1 slice dried whole
    wheat bread
1   tablespoon fresh lemon juice
    Salt and freshly ground pepper to taste

1. Preheat oven to 375° F.

2. Cut zucchinis in half lengthwise and carefully remove pulp, keeping about ¼ inch of shell intact. Put pulp in a small mixing bowl and set aside. Place zucchini shells side by side on a small baking sheet lightly coated with vegetable spray and set aside.

3. Heat olive oil in a nonstick skillet. Add shallot and cook over medium heat for 3 minutes, stirring often.

4. Add zucchini pulp, water chestnuts, parsley, and wine to skillet and bring to a boil. Lower heat, stir in flour and cook for 2 minutes or until mixture starts to thicken.

Remove from heat, stir in bread crumbs and lemon juice and season to taste with salt and pepper.

5. Spoon mixture from skillet into zucchini shells on baking sheet, mounding slightly. Spray tops lightly with cooking oil and bake for 15 minutes. Serve immediately.

MAKES 8 STUFFED ZUCCHINI HALVES V

PER ZUCCHINI HALF: 35 CALORIES; 1.1 GRAMS PROTEIN; 5.1 GRAMS CARBOHYDRATES; 1.4 GRAMS FAT; 0 MILLIGRAMS CHOLESTEROL; 5 MILLIGRAMS SODIUM (WITHOUT SALTING).

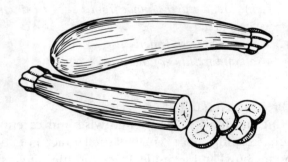

◆ ◆ ◆ ◆ ◆

VEGETABLE KEBABS

▶ ▶

Traditionally, shish kebabs are chunks of marinated meat, poultry, or fish and vegetables that are threaded on a skewer and grilled or broiled. Here, we drop the meat entirely and concentrate exclusively on vegetables to produce a thoroughly satisfying and dramatic dish.

An excellent starter, it can also be stretched by doubling the recipe and serving it over rice as an entrée. To make this recipe vegan, eliminate the cheese.

2	*small yellow squash, cut into ½-inch pieces*
2	*small zucchini, cut into ½-inch pieces*
8	*small mushroom caps, wiped clean*
4	*cherry tomatoes*
¼	*cup Fat-Free Vinaigrette Dressing (page 9)*
1	*tablespoon grated low fat Parmesan or Romano cheese*

1. Place vegetables in a bowl and add vinaigrette. Gently toss to combine, and allow vegetables to marinate for about 2 hours.

2. Preheat broiler or prepare grill.

3. Thread vegetables alternately and evenly on 4 skewers and broil or grill, turning skewers once, for 5 to 7 minutes or until vegetables are crisp-tender. Sprinkle kebabs with grated cheese and serve hot.

SERVES 4

PER SERVING: 23 CALORIES; 1.7 GRAMS PROTEIN; 3.4 GRAMS
CARBOHYDRATES; .4 GRAMS FAT; 1 MILLIGRAM CHOLESTEROL;
25 MILLIGRAMS SODIUM (WITHOUT SALTING).

◆ ◆ ◆ ◆ ◆

CAULIFLOWER WITH CUCUMBER-YOGURT DIP

▶ ▶

Mark Twain once noted, "Cauliflower is nothing but cabbage with a college education." And here we have it paired with cucumber in a yogurt-based dressing for an appetizer that is both smart *and* cultured. It just doesn't get better than that!

1	*medium head cauliflower*
1	*cup low fat plain yogurt*
1	*small cucumber, peeled and diced*
1	*clove garlic, pressed*
½	*teaspoon ground cumin*
	Pinch cayenne pepper or to taste
	Salt and freshly ground pepper to taste

1. Separate cauliflower into bite-size florets, arrange on a serving dish, and set aside.

2. Combine all remaining ingredients in a bowl and mix thoroughly. Place dip beside cauliflower and serve.

SERVES 6

PER SERVING: 35 CALORIES; 2.7 GRAMS PROTEIN; 4.6 GRAMS CARBOHYDRATES; .7 GRAMS FAT; 2.3 MILLIGRAMS CHOLESTEROL; 35 MILLIGRAMS SODIUM (WITHOUT SALTING).

◆ ◆ ◆ ◆

EGGPLANT RUMANIAN

▶ ▶

Eggplant is commonly thought of as a vegetable. However, eggplant is actually a fruit . . . a berry, to be exact! A terrific source of potassium and folic acid, it is highly regarded by cooks from all over the world.

In this versatile recipe, the eggplant can be used as a spread on crackers or pita triangles, or served on individual dishes as an appetizer or starter spooned over lettuce and garnished with tomato, scallions, and cucumber slices.

> 1   eggplant, about 1 pound
> 1   medium onion, diced
> 2   tablespoons chopped fresh cilantro or parsley
> ¼   cup Vegetable Stock (page 19) or canned no-salt-added broth
> 2   teaspoons olive oil
>   Juice of 1 lemon
> ¼   teaspoon thyme
> ¼   teaspoon hot pepper flakes (optional)
>   Salt and freshly ground pepper to taste

1. Preheat oven to 350° F.

2. Pierce eggplant in two or three places and set on a flat, nonstick baking pan. Bake for 20 to 30 minutes or until eggplant is tender. Remove from oven and let cool.

3. Remove stem from eggplant and peel. Roughly chop pulp, place in a bowl and stir in onion and cilantro or parsley. Add all remaining ingredients and mix until thoroughly combined. Chill at least 1 hour before serving.

SERVES 6 V

PER SERVING: 40 CALORIES; .9 GRAMS PROTEIN; 5.8 GRAMS CARBOHYDRATES; 1.6 GRAMS FAT; 0 MILLIGRAMS CHOLESTEROL; 10 MILLIGRAMS SODIUM (WITHOUT SALTING).

◆ ◆ ◆ ◆ ◆

TANGY CARROTS
AND DAIKON

▶ ▶

Because both the daikon and carrots are presented in their raw state, you will benefit from the maximum nutrients available. Scallions add dash, flavor, and color contrast. Sauced with a Japanese-type vinaigrette, this dish makes a handsome starter to an Oriental-inspired dinner or as a salad side dish.

If daikon is not available, try black radish or use the more common red-skinned radish.

4   *medium carrots, grated*
1   *cup grated daikon radish*
4   *scallions, with tops, minced*
½   *cup rice wine vinegar*
½   *tablespoon sesame oil*
1   *tablespoon minced fresh basil or ½ tablespoon dried*

1. Combine carrots, daikon, and scallion in a bowl and mix thoroughly.

2. In a separate bowl, combine vinegar and oil. Stir until well blended and spoon mixture over vegetables. Toss until vegetables are coated with dressing.

3. Spoon carrot-daikon mixture into a serving dish and sprinkle with basil before serving.

SERVES 6 V

PER SERVING: 36 CALORIES; .6 GRAMS PROTEIN; 5.9 GRAMS CARBOHYDRATES; 1.2 GRAMS FAT; 0 MILLIGRAMS CHOLESTEROL; 20 MILLIGRAMS SODIUM (WITHOUT SALTING).

◆ ◆ ◆ ◆ ◆

ROASTED GARLIC AND CHICK-PEA SPREAD

▶ ▶

Do not be afraid of this recipe because of the quantity of garlic. Roasting the garlic takes out the "bite" and the resulting taste acts as the perfect foil for the mild, nutlike flavor of chick-peas.

The spread's slightly chunky texture makes it a natural with pita or toast triangles, no-salt tortilla chips, or as an unexpected stuffing for cherry tomatoes, celery, or endive leaves. Use also as a dip for your favorite crudités.

1   *whole bud garlic (about 14 cloves), separated*
    Vegetable oil cooking spray
2   *cups canned chick-peas, no-salt-added or very*
    well rinsed, drained
1   *small onion, quartered*
    Juice from 2 medium lemons
    Paprika to taste

1. Preheat oven to 375° F.
2. Place unpeeled garlic cloves on a small baking sheet or dish and spray lightly with cooking oil. Bake for about 20 minutes or until garlic is tender (test for softness with tip of a small, sharp knife or a sturdy toothpick). Do not let garlic brown. Remove from oven and let cool slightly. Slip off skins and trim ends.
3. Place garlic pulp and all remaining ingredients, except paprika, in a food processor and process until coarsely puréed.

4. Transfer mixture to a serving bowl and sprinkle lightly with paprika.

MAKES ABOUT 2 CUPS V

PER TABLESPOON: 15 CALORIES; .7 GRAMS PROTEIN; 3.1 GRAMS CARBOHYDRATES; .1 GRAM FAT; 0 MILLIGRAMS CHOLESTEROL; 2 MILLIGRAMS SODIUM (WITHOUT SALTING).

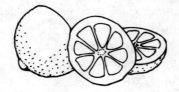

◆ ◆ ◆ ◆

BAKED
HOT POTATO CHIPS

▶▶▶▶▶▶▶▶▶▶▶▶▶▶▶▶▶▶▶▶▶▶▶▶▶

This simple recipe is one of my all-time favorites. Greaseless, golden-brown disks of good health and great taste. Variations abound: sweet potatoes may be substituted for the white baking potatoes, and you may use either sweet or hot paprika, chili powder, or cayenne pepper, or your favorite dried herb for a sensational premeal and side-dish treat. I also like to bake up a batch of these chips for a satisfying low-cal, low fat snack.

Vegetable oil cooking spray
2   *large baking potatoes, thinly sliced*
2   *teaspoons vegetable oil*
    Salt and freshly ground pepper to taste
    Hot paprika to taste

1. Preheat oven to 350° F.

2. Lightly coat a nonstick baking sheet with cooking spray. Place potato slices on the baking sheet, brush potatoes with oil and season with salt and pepper.

3. Bake about 10 minutes, or until potatoes are golden brown and tender. Remove from oven, sprinkle with paprika, and serve hot.

SERVES 4 V

PER SERVING: 90 CALORIES; 1.7 GRAMS PROTEIN; 15.1 GRAMS CARBOHYDRATES; 2.9 GRAMS FAT; 0 MILLIGRAMS CHOLESTEROL; 5 MILLIGRAMS SODIUM (WITHOUT SALTING).

◆ ◆ ◆ ◆ ◆

APPLES AND TOFU
WITH SESAME SEED DRESSING

▶ ▶

Cool and crunchy with a curiously spunky yet mild flavor, this lovely, unusual starter with its Oriental overtones will make your guests sit up and take notice.

3   *Granny Smith or other tart apples, cored and*
    thinly sliced
4   *ounces medium-firm tofu, well drained and cubed*
2   *stalks celery, chopped*
6   *large lettuce leaves*
2   *tablespoons rice wine vinegar*
2   *tablespoons low fat egg-free mayonnaise*
2   *teaspoons toasted sesame seeds*
    Salt and freshly ground pepper to taste

1. Combine apples, tofu, and celery, and gently toss with vinegar.

2. Place a lettuce leaf on each of four individual serving plates. Mound tofu mixture in center of each leaf.

3. Combine mayonnaise and sesame seeds. Mix well and spoon over apple-tofu mixture.

SERVES 6 V

PER SERVING: 75 CALORIES; 2.0 GRAMS PROTEIN; 10.7 GRAMS CARBOHYDRATES; 2.5 GRAMS FAT; 0 MILLIGRAMS CHOLESTEROL; 25 MILLIGRAMS SODIUM (WITHOUT SALTING).

◆ ◆ ◆ ◆

TOMATOES PROVENÇAL
WITH MOZZARELLA

▶▶▶▶▶▶▶▶▶▶▶▶▶▶▶▶▶▶▶▶▶▶▶▶

This tomato dish is a fine prelude to any tomato-sauce-less pasta, pilaf, or polenta-powered meal. If fresh basil is unavailable, use the always-present fresh parsley.

4 large just-ripe tomatoes, trimmed and cut
   crosswise into ¼-inch slices
2 cloves garlic, pressed
3 teaspoons red wine vinegar
½ tablespoon olive oil
2 tablespoons chopped fresh basil or Italian parsley
1 teaspoon dried oregano
   Salt and freshly ground pepper to taste
1 ounce low fat mozzarella, shredded

1. Preheat oven to 350° F.

2. Place tomato slices on a shallow nonstick baking pan, allowing them to overlap slightly.

3. Combine garlic, vinegar, and oil in a jar with a tight-fitting lid and shake until very well blended. Brush or spoon garlic mixture over tomatoes, sprinkle evenly with parsley, oregano, salt and pepper, and mozzarella.

4. Bake for 15 minutes and serve immediately.

SERVES 6

PER SERVING: 40 CALORIES; 2.0 GRAMS PROTEIN; 4.6 GRAMS CARBOHYDRATES; 2.0 GRAMS FAT; 1.7 MILLIGRAMS CHOLESTEROL; 50 MILLIGRAMS SODIUM (WITHOUT SALTING).

LIGHT MEALS and SALADS

ONION AND
WILD MUSHROOM PIE

◆◆◆◆◆

▶ ▶

Imagine the biggest, best potato pancake you've ever had, then think how glorious it would taste if it was complemented by a tasty topping. Well, that will give you an inkling of the delicious and unusual pie crust—and filling—outlined below. Once you've gotten the gist of the techniques employed here, you may want to create your own topping combinations.

Accompany with a salad of bitter greens (arugula, chicory, radicchio, endive, etc.) sprinkled with pomegranate seeds or dried sour cherries or cranberries, tossed with my Fat-Free Vinaigrette Dressing (page 9) using raspberry vinegar.

POTATO CRUST
Vegetable oil cooking spray
2 *medium potatoes, peeled and quartered*
1 *medium onion, peeled and quartered*
2 *tablespoons unbleached all-purpose flour*
Egg substitute equal to 1 egg or 1 large egg
Salt and freshly ground black pepper to taste

FILLING
1 *tablespoon olive oil*
1 *large Spanish onion, thinly sliced*
¾ *pound fresh wild mushrooms (oyster, porcini, and/or Chanterelle, etc.), trimmed, wiped clean, and thinly sliced*

¼ pound white mushrooms, trimmed, wiped clean,
    and thinly sliced
    Salt and freshly ground pepper to taste
1 teaspoon dried thyme
1 teaspoon dry mustard
2 tablespoons flour
¼ cup dry white wine
¼ cup water
2 tablespoons minced fresh parsley
2 tablespoons grated low fat Parmesan cheese

1. Preheat oven to 350° F. Lightly coat a 10-inch pie plate with vegetable spray and set aside.

2. Grate potatoes and onion in food processor. Transfer to a mixing bowl and squeeze out as much liquid as possible. Add remaining crust ingredients to potato-onion mixture and stir until well blended. Spoon into prepared pie plate, using back of spoon to spread mixture evenly over bottom and up to sides, but not rim of pan. Bake in oven for 20 minutes. Remove from oven and set aside to cool slightly.

3. While crust bakes, prepare filling: Heat oil in a large nonstick skillet. Add onions and cook over medium heat, stirring often, for 5 minutes, or until onions are lightly golden. Add mushrooms and cook an additional 5 minutes.

4. Sprinkle salt, pepper, thyme, mustard, and flour over onion-mushroom mixture and stir to blend well. Add wine and water and bring to a boil, stirring constantly. Reduce heat and let simmer for 2 or 3 minutes or until thickened. Taste and adjust seasonings if necessary.

5. Spoon mixture from skillet onto baked potato crust and spread evenly. Mix parsley with cheese and sprinkle over top. Return to oven and bake for 15 minutes.

6. Remove from oven, let stand for about 5 minutes, then cut into wedges and serve.

SERVES 6

PER SERVING: 135 CALORIES; 5.3 GRAMS PROTEIN; 21.5 GRAMS CARBOHYDRATES; 3.6 GRAMS FAT; .9 MILLIGRAMS CHOLESTEROL; 50 MILLIGRAMS SODIUM (WITHOUT SALTING).

◆ ◆ ◆ ◆ ◆

ARTICHOKE
AND LEEK PIE

▶ ▶

Although the crust may be made in advance of the filling, it should not be frozen or it will get "mushy." The addition of artichoke hearts to leeks, onions, garlic, and homemade bread crumbs gives this pie a fulsome, hardy taste so I like to serve it with just a simple salad of sliced tomatoes.

1	Potato Crust (page 59)
1	tablespoon olive oil
1	small onion, minced
3	medium leeks, white and tender greens, well rinsed and sliced
1	clove garlic, minced
1	9-ounce package frozen artichoke hearts, thawed and quartered
1	cup bread crumbs, made from 2 slices dried and lightly toasted whole wheat bread
1	tablespoon flour
3	tablespoons low fat (2%) milk
	Salt and freshly ground pepper to taste

1. Prepare crust and bake 20 minutes, remove from oven and let cool slightly. Do not turn off oven.

2. While crust bakes, prepare filling: Heat oil in a large nonstick skillet. Add onion, leeks, and garlic and stir over medium heat for 2 minutes. Reduce heat to very low, cover and simmer gently for 5 minutes.

3. Add artichoke hearts, ½ cup of the bread crumbs, and

salt and pepper to taste. Dissolve flour in milk and stir into skillet. Stir over medium-high heat until mixture starts to thicken. Remove from heat, let cool slightly, taste and adjust seasonings if necessary.

4. Transfer contents of skillet to pie crust and sprinkle top with remaining bread crumbs. Bake for 15 minutes. Let stand a few minutes before serving.

SERVES 6

PER SERVING: 175 CALORIES; 5.9 GRAMS PROTEIN; 30.9 GRAMS CARBOHYDRATES; .5 GRAMS FAT; 0 MILLIGRAMS CHO-LESTEROL; 110 MILLIGRAMS SODIUM (WITHOUT SALTING).

◆ ◆ ◆ ◆ ◆

THAI-MARINADED
GRILLED TOFU

▶ ▶

Custard-like tofu is made from curdled soy milk, an iron-rich liquid extracted from cooked, ground soybeans. The resulting curds are drained and pressed. Its firmness depends on how much whey has been pressed out.

Tofu is very perishable and should be refrigerated and stored covered with water, which must be changed daily. In this tasty recipe, the tofu needs to be marinated for at least twenty-four hours . . . ideally for two or three days. The spiced lime-juice marinade creates a sensational infusion for these tofu-tiles.

Serve on a bed of greens or cubed in pita pockets with shreds of lettuce, tomatoes, chopped onions, minced cilantro, and/or diced cucumbers.

1	*12-ounce block medium-firm tofu, well drained*
1½	*cups warm water*
3	*tablespoons fresh lime juice*
2	*teaspoons sesame oil*
2	*large cloves garlic, pressed*
6	*scallions, white bulb and tender greens, chopped*
2	*teaspoons freshly grated ginger*
1	*tablespoon minced fresh mint or ½ tablespoon dried*
	Hot pepper flakes to taste

1. Cut tofu block in thirds, then into ¼-inch slabs. Place tofu in a shallow bowl, and set aside.

---

2. Combine all remaining ingredients in a separate bowl and blend thoroughly. Pour marinade over sliced tofu, cover tightly, and refrigerate for at least 24 hours, turning once or twice.

3. Prepare grill or broiler.

4. Grill or broil tofu until grill marks appear or until browned. Turn carefully, brush with any leftover marinade and grill other side until nicely browned.

SERVES 4 V

PER SERVING: 95 CALORIES; 7.2 GRAMS PROTEIN; 3.7 GRAMS CARBOHYDRATES; 6.5 GRAMS FAT; 0 MILLIGRAMS CHOLESTEROL; 20 MILLIGRAMS SODIUM (WITHOUT SALTING).

◆ ◆ ◆ ◆ ◆

TURNIP AND
ZUCCHINI BAKE

▶ ▶

This earthy casserole is a perfect meal on its own and needs only a pitcher of apple cider, iced tea, or coffee along for the ride.

If you wish to make this recipe completely vegan, substitute a sprinkling of grated bread crumbs for the shredded cheese.

	Vegetable oil cooking spray
2	*small turnips, thinly sliced*
2	*medium zucchini, sliced*
1	*large onion, sliced*
2	*green or red bell peppers, cored, seeded, and sliced*
4	*just-ripe plum tomatoes, quartered*
½	*cup low sodium vegetable juice*
	Salt and freshly ground pepper to taste
1	*ounce low fat Swiss cheese, shredded*

1. Lightly coat a nonstick skillet with cooking spray. Add turnips, zucchini, onion, and bell peppers to skillet, and cook over medium heat, stirring occasionally, for 5 minutes.

2. Add tomatoes and vegetable juice to skillet. Cover, reduce heat to low, and simmer gently, stirring occasionally, for about 10 minutes or until turnips are tender.

3. Preheat broiler while vegetables cook.

4. Season vegetables to taste and transfer to an oven-proof baking dish or casserole. Sprinkle cheese on top and

broil about 5 minutes or until cheese bubbles and is lightly browned. Serve immediately.

SERVES 4

PER SERVING: 100 CALORIES; 5.2 GRAMS PROTEIN; 16.2 GRAMS CARBOHYDRATES; 2.8 GRAMS FAT; 3.7 MILLIGRAMS CHOLESTEROL; 90 MILLIGRAMS SODIUM (WITHOUT SALTING).

◆ ◆ ◆ ◆ ◆

POTATO, PEPPER, AND FENNEL PANACHE

▶ ▶

This recipe is not only attractive, with its combination of colors, but delivers goodly amounts of potassium, vitamin A, and vitamin C.

2 *medium red-skinned potatoes, cooked and sliced*
2 *red bell peppers, roasted (page 76, step 1), sliced lengthwise*
2 *small fennel bulbs*
   Fresh ground pepper to taste
3 *teaspoons vegetable oil*
2 *teaspoons fennel seeds*
½ *cup low sodium tomato juice*
¼ *teaspoon dried thyme*
   Salt to taste

1. Preheat broiler.

2. Arrange potato and roasted red pepper slices on a serving platter and set aside.

3. Trim fennel and cut each bulb into ½-inch slices. Place fennel in a shallow baking pan, sprinkle with pepper and brush with 2 teaspoons of the oil. Broil for 5 to 8 minutes or until fennel is just tender. Allow fennel to cool for 5 minutes, then add to serving platter with potatoes and peppers and sprinkle with fennel seeds.

4. Combine remaining teaspoon oil with tomato juice, thyme, and salt if desired. Mix until well blended and spoon over vegetables on platter.

SERVES 4 V

PER SERVING: 105 CALORIES; 2.5 GRAMS PROTEIN; 15.7 GRAMS CARBOHYDRATES; 3.8 GRAMS FAT; 0 MILLIGRAMS CHOLESTEROL; 60 MILLIGRAMS SODIUM (WITHOUT SALTING).

POTATO AND
SPRING VEGETABLE
FRITTATA

▶ ▶

Basically, a frittata is an omelet with an Italian accent. Frittatas usually have the ingredients mixed with the eggs rather than folded inside as with French omelets. It can be flipped or finished under the broiler, and because it's cooked more slowly over medium-low heat, frittatas are firmer than omelets cooked over high heat after folding.

This frittata, chock-a-block with all kinds of good stuff, does not require many eggs—just enough to hold ingredients together, which is easily accomplished with an egg substitute. Once you get the hang of it, it's fun to create your own frittata fixings. Perfect with a pitcher of fresh lemonade, iced espresso, or tea.

1	*pound new potatoes, unpeeled*
1	*tablespoon margarine*
1	*medium onion, thinly sliced*
5	*thin stalks asparagus, trimmed of tough ends, sliced, and blanched*
½	*cup corn kernels, fresh or frozen and thawed*
½	*cup petite green peas, fresh or frozen and thawed*
	Egg substitute equal to 4 eggs or 2 large eggs and 2 egg whites
3	*tablespoons water*

1. Boil potatoes until just tender, and dice. Heat marga-

rine in a large nonstick skillet and add onion. Sauté until onion is quite soft.

2. Add potatoes, raise heat slightly and cook until potatoes are just showing flecks of gold. Stir in asparagus, corn, and peas and cook for 2 minutes.

3. Whisk eggs with water and pour over mixture in skillet. Cook over medium heat, shaking skillet occasionally and lifting mixture with a spatula, until eggs set and brown lightly on the bottom.

4. Remove skillet from heat, cover with a large plate, invert skillet and slide egg mixture onto plate. Return skillet to stove and slide frittata (now turned over) back into skillet. Cook, shaking skillet occasionally, until mixture is cooked through. If you wish, you can begin the frittata in an oven-proof skillet on the stove, then transfer skillet to preheated broiler to finish cooking.

5. Slide frittata onto a warmed platter, cut into wedges, and serve.

SERVES 6

PER SERVING: 105 CALORIES; 6.0 GRAMS PROTEIN; 16.6 GRAMS CARBOHYDRATES; 2.1 GRAMS FAT; 0 MILLIGRAMS CHOLESTEROL; 80 MILLIGRAMS SODIUM (WITHOUT SALTING).

♦ ♦ ♦ ♦ ♦

PASTA FRITTATA

▶ ▶

If you have some leftover tomato-based pasta sauce, use it instead of the sauce outlined below (my Arribiata on page 91 makes a wonderful frittata). Serve with hot crusty bread and a green salad tossed lightly with olive oil, fresh lemon juice, and salt.

½   tablespoon olive oil
2   cloves garlic, chopped, or to taste
4   pitted black olives, thinly sliced
1   tablespoon rinsed and drained capers (optional)
¼   teaspoon dried crushed hot red pepper flakes
2   cups chopped, canned plum tomatoes, drained
     Pinch dried oregano
     Salt and freshly ground pepper to taste
⅓   pound penne or other tubular pasta, cooked al
     dente
2   teaspoons margarine
     Egg substitute equal to 4 eggs, or 2 eggs and 2 egg
     whites
3   tablespoons water

1. Heat olive oil in a large, nonstick skillet and sauté garlic with olives, capers, and hot pepper flakes until garlic is soft and barely golden.

2. Raise heat to high and add tomatoes all at once. Stir in oregano, reduce heat, and simmer tomatoes for 10 minutes. Taste and add salt and pepper.

3. Add pasta to skillet and stir to coat well with sauce.

(Pasta can be prepared one day ahead and refrigerated, well covered. Bring mixture to room temperature before proceeding with recipe.)

4. Transfer pasta mixture to a bowl, wipe out skillet, and add margarine. Whisk eggs with water and pour into skillet. Cook eggs for 1 minute over medium heat, then add pasta mixture to skillet. Do not stir, but lift edges of frittata with a spatula to allow some egg mixture to dribble to the bottom. Cook until bottom is set and lightly golden.

5. Remove skillet from heat, cover with a large plate, invert skillet and slide egg mixture onto plate. Return skillet to stove and slide frittata (now turned over) back into skillet. Cook, shaking skillet occasionally, until mixture is cooked through. If you wish, you can begin the frittata in an oven-proof skillet on the stove, then transfer skillet to preheated broiler to finish cooking.

6. Slide frittata onto a warmed platter, cut into wedges, and serve hot.

SERVES 6

PER SERVING: 152 CALORIES; 7.3 GRAMS PROTEIN; 23.4 GRAMS CARBOHYDRATES; 3.1 GRAMS FAT; 0 MILLIGRAMS CHOLESTEROL; 140 MILLIGRAMS SODIUM (WITHOUT SALTING).

WARM FUSILLI
AND SUN-DRIED TOMATO SALAD

◆◆◆◆◆

▶▶▶▶▶▶▶▶▶▶▶▶▶▶▶▶▶▶▶▶▶▶

Sun-dried tomatoes tossed with romaine, fresh lemon juice, and oil create the perfect frame for vegetable spirals and mozzarella topped with just-grated Parmesan or Romano. To complete the picture, serve with toasted Italian garlic bread.

¼   cup unseasoned sun-dried tomatoes, plumped in hot water
1   tablespoon hot olive oil
½   pound vegetable (tricolor) fusilli or spiral pasta
1   ounce low fat mozzarella cheese, shredded
2   tablespoons fresh lemon juice
    Salt (optional)
2   cups torn romaine lettuce leaves
2   tablespoons grated low fat Parmesan or Romano cheese
    Freshly ground pepper to taste (optional)

1. Drain sun-dried tomatoes and chop coarsely. Combine tomatoes with hot oil and set aside to soak for 10 minutes.

2. Cook pasta until tender. Drain, let cool slightly and toss briefly with mozzarella and salt, if desired.

3. While pasta cools, drain the sun-dried tomatoes, reserving oil; set aside tomatoes. Whisk together the oil from the tomatoes with lemon juice.

4. Toss romaine with sun-dried tomatoes and oil-lemon

juice mixture. Divide lettuce among four plates and top with equal portions of pasta and grated Parmesan or Romano. Top each portion with several grindings of pepper, if desired, and serve.

SERVES 4
PER SERVING: 290 CALORIES; 11.5 GRAMS PROTEIN; 48.0 GRAMS CARBOHYDRATES; 5.8 GRAMS FAT; 3.9 MILLIGRAMS CHOLESTEROL; 110 MILLIGRAMS SODIUM (WITHOUT SALTING).

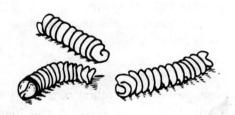

♦ ♦ ♦ ♦ ♦

CELLOPHANE NOODLES
WITH ROASTED RED PEPPER PURÉE

▶ ▶

Cellophane noodles, made from ground mung beans, are hard and opaque white before cooking and become translucent and slippery when cooked. They have more texture than flavor and absorb other flavors easily.

2   *large red bell peppers*
3   *cups Vegetable Stock (page 19) or canned low*
    sodium broth
6   *cups water*
½   *pound cellophane noodles*
⅛   *teaspoon ground Szechuan pepper to taste*
    (optional)
    Salt to taste

1. Place peppers on a broiling pan and broil, turning frequently, until skin is well charred and black. Transfer peppers to a paper bag. Close bag and let stand until just cool enough to handle. When peppers have cooled, scrape away charred skin under cold running water until peppers are completely peeled. Core and seed peppers.

2. Cut peppers into large pieces and place in a food processor. Add 1 cup stock and process until peppers are smoothly puréed. Spoon purée into a bowl and reserve.

3. Bring water to a boil in a saucepan. Add noodles and cook for 15 minutes. Drain noodles, rinse with cold water, then drain again.

4. Return noodles to empty saucepan, add remaining

stock and simmer until ingredients are hot. Add red pepper purée and Szechuan pepper, if desired, and toss to combine ingredients. Taste and adjust seasonings, if necessary. Transfer to serving dish and serve hot.

SERVES 4 V

PER SERVING: 230 CALORIES; .9 GRAMS PROTEIN; 55.0 GRAMS CARBOHYDRATES; .5 GRAMS FAT; 0 MILLIGRAMS CHOLESTEROL; 55 MILLIGRAMS SODIUM (WITHOUT SALTING).

♦ ♦ ♦ ♦

QUINOA SALAD

▷ ▶ ▷ ▶ ▷ ▶ ▷ ▶ ▷ ▶ ▷ ▶ ▷ ▶ ▷ ▶ ▷ ▶ ▷ ▶ ▷

The ancient Incas called quinoa (KEEN-wah) "the mother grain"—perhaps because they sensed it contained more protein than any other grain. Speck-sized and bead-shaped, ivory-colored quinoa cooks like rice (but in half the time) and expands to four times its original volume. Comparable to couscous in flavor, quinoa is terrific as part of a main dish, side dish, soups, puddings, and salads.

Begin with Vegetable Stock (page 19) cooked with added vegetables for a tasty and hearty light lunch.

2   cups water
1   cup quinoa
1   large cucumber, peeled, seeded, and diced
2   just-ripe plum tomatoes, seeded and diced
1   medium onion, diced
1   small stalk celery, diced
1   small green pepper, trimmed and diced
2   tablespoons minced jalapeño pepper or to
     taste
⅓   cup minced fresh cilantro
¼   cup fresh lime or lemon juice
1   tablespoon sesame oil
2   teaspoons low sodium soy sauce
     Salt and freshly ground pepper to taste

1. Bring water to boil and add quinoa. Reduce heat to low, cover, and simmer, stirring occasionally, for about 15 minutes or until quinoa is tender. Remove from heat and let

stand, covered, for 5 minutes. Transfer quinoa to a large bowl and cool to room temperature.

2. Add cucumber, tomatoes, onion, celery, green and jalapeño peppers, and cilantro to quinoa. Toss gently to blend.

3. Combine remaining ingredients in a separate bowl and stir to blend thoroughly. Pour onto quinoa-vegetable mix and toss gently until ingredients are coated with dressing and well blended.

SERVES 4 V

PER SERVING: 230 CALORIES; 6.9 GRAMS PROTEIN; 39.4 GRAMS CARBOHYDRATES; 6.0 GRAMS FAT; 0 MILLIGRAMS CHOLESTEROL; 120 MILLIGRAMS SODIUM (WITHOUT SALTING).

◆ ◆ ◆ ◆ ◆

BROWN RICE
AND VEGETABLE SALAD

▶ ▶

A riot of color, the crunch of fresh radish, celery, zucchini, olives, pimiento, peas all nestled in brown rice makes this Provençal-inspired salad a marvelous light lunch or supper, or a side dish for dinner. Serve with garlic toast or multigrain bread.

3	cups cooked brown rice
4	scallions, white and tender greens, finely sliced
4	radishes, finely sliced
1	stalk celery, diced
1	small zucchini, trimmed and diced
4	pitted black olives, rinsed and thinly sliced
3	tablespoons diced pimientos
¾	cup frozen green peas, boiled and drained
¼	cup chopped fresh Italian parsley
¼	cup red wine vinegar
¼	cup Vegetable Stock (page 19) or canned low sodium broth
2	tablespoons olive oil
1	clove garlic, pressed
	Salt and freshly ground pepper to taste
12	large romaine lettuce leaves

1. In a large mixing bowl combine rice with vegetables and parsley and toss to blend.

2. Mix vinegar, stock, oil, and garlic and pour over rice-vegetable mixture. Season to taste with salt and pepper and

toss gently to blend ingredients. Cover and refrigerate or let stand at room temperature for about 15 minutes, tossing occasionally.

3. To serve, place 3 lettuce leaves on chilled individual serving plates and top with equal amounts of rice-vegetable mixture.

SERVES 4 V

PER SERVING: 260 CALORIES; 5.9 GRAMS PROTEIN; 42.8 GRAMS CARBOHYDRATES; 6.1 GRAMS FAT; 0 MILLIGRAMS CHOLESTEROL; 90 MILLIGRAMS SODIUM (WITHOUT SALTING).

◆ ◆ ◆ ◆

MANY BEAN SALAD
WITH SHERRY MARINADE

▶ ▶

Aside from being a powerhouse of nutrition, this four-bean salad can be quick and easy to prepare because the legumes used can be canned. And, since recent studies have shown that canning does *not* diminish the nutritive value of food to any great degree, you'll still be ahead of the game. Notice, too, the salad calls for no-salt-added or well-rinsed canned beans to keep the sodium content in check.

Doled out on lettuce-leaf cups, it makes a wonderful light lunch.

> 1 *cup cooked red kidney beans, or canned (no-salt-added or well-rinsed and drained)*
> 1 *cup cooked white beans, or canned (no-salt-added or well-rinsed and drained)*
> 1 *cup cooked black beans, or canned (no-salt-added or well-rinsed and drained)*
> ½ *pound green beans, steamed and cut into 1-inch lengths*
> 1 *small red onion, minced*
> 1 *small red bell pepper, trimmed and diced*
> 2 *tablespoons finely minced fresh parsley*

SHERRY MARINADE
> ¼ *cup red wine vinegar*
> ¼ *cup Vegetable Stock (page 19) or canned low sodium broth*
> 2 *tablespoons dry sherry (not cooking sherry)*

---

1   clove garlic, pressed
1   tablespoon olive oil
    Salt and freshly ground pepper to taste

1. In a large mixing bowl, combine beans with onion, bell pepper, and parsley. Toss gently to avoid breaking beans.
2. Combine marinade ingredients and stir well. Pour dressing over beans and vegetables and toss very gently, just to coat beans. Cover and refrigerate for at least 1 hour to allow flavors to blend.

SERVES 6 V
PER SERVING: 185 CALORIES; 8.9 GRAMS PROTEIN; 26.5 GRAMS CARBOHYDRATES; 5.0 GRAMS FAT; 0 MILLIGRAMS CHOLESTEROL; 10 MILLIGRAMS SODIUM (WITHOUT SALTING).

◆ ◆ ◆ ◆ ◆

HOT POTATO SALAD

▶ ▶

For this recipe I let the celery and scallions stand in a bit of hot stock for ten minutes—just time enough to warm them up without losing all the taste and crunch.

1½ *pounds small red or new, thin-skinned potatoes, unpeeled*
1 *large stalk celery, diced*
½ *cup finely diced scallions, white and tender greens*
¼ *cup hot Vegetable Stock (page 19), canned low sodium broth, or water*
1 *tablespoon olive oil*
3 *tablespoons balsamic vinegar*
2 *teaspoons prepared coarse mustard (optional)*
3 *tablespoons finely chopped fresh parsley*
  Salt and freshly ground pepper to taste

1. Boil potatoes until just tender.

2. While potatoes cook, combine celery and scallions in a large bowl and cover with hot stock or water. Let stand 10 minutes, then whisk in oil, vinegar, and mustard, if desired.

3. When potatoes are done, drain well, cut in halves, and toss quickly in oil and vinegar mixture along with parsley. Taste and adjust seasonings, if necessary. Serve hot.

SERVES 4 V

PER SERVING: 150 CALORIES; 3.3 GRAMS PROTEIN; 25.5 GRAMS CARBOHYDRATES; 4.0 GRAMS FAT; 0 MILLIGRAMS CHOLESTEROL; 25 MILLIGRAMS SODIUM (WITHOUT SALTING).

◆ ◆ ◆ ◆ ◆

ASPARAGUS AND ENDIVE SALAD WITH LEMON VINAIGRETTE

▶▶▶▶▶▶▶▶▶▶▶▶▶▶▶▶▶▶▶▶▶▶▶▶▶

Add this wonderful vinaigrette to your list of fat-free sauces and your salads will be very tastefully dressed. It is a perfect match with this elegant salad of endive and the universally popular asparagus. If the edible portion of asparagus stems are tough, remove the outer layer with a vegetable peeler or good paring knife.

For a delightful and sophisticated luncheon, try this salad along with graceful sandwiches containing thin disks of cucumber on crustless seven-grain bread cut into small squares.

4   heads endive
1   pound asparagus, trimmed of tough ends,
    steamed and chilled
4   teaspoons chopped chives

LEMON VINAIGRETTE
4   tablespoons rice wine vinegar
1   tablespoon fresh lemon juice
½   tablespoon grated lemon rind
1   teaspoon sugar
    Salt and freshly ground pepper to taste

1. Separate each endive into individual leaves and arrange leaves on four serving plates. Divide asparagus into four portions and arrange over endive leaves.

2. Combine all vinaigrette ingredients in a jar with a

---

tight-fitting lid. Cover and shake until well blended. Spoon mixture over asparagus and endive, sprinkle each serving with a teaspoon of chives, and serve.

SERVES 4 V

PER SERVING: 30 CALORIES; 2.4 GRAMS PROTEIN; 5.4 GRAMS CARBOHYDRATES; .1 GRAM FAT; 0 MILLIGRAMS CHOLESTEROL; 10 MILLIGRAMS SODIUM (WITHOUT SALTING).

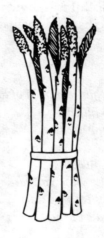

GRAPEFRUIT AND JICAMA SALAD
WITH MELON

▶▶▶▶▶▶▶▶▶▶▶▶▶▶▶▶▶▶▶▶▶▶▶▶▶▶

Jicama (HEE-kah-mah) is often referred to as the Mexican potato, perhaps because it boasts similar versatility and similar nutrients—namely vitamin C and potassium. However, the comparison ends there because the jicama has a sweet, nutty flavor and may be enjoyed both raw and cooked. It can be stored in the refrigerator for up to five days, and the thin skin should be peeled just before using.

You will find jicama in Mexican markets and most large supermarkets. Because its texture resembles the crisp water chestnut or the delicious Japanese radish (daikon), either may be substituted if jicama is unavailable.

Here, jicama joins forces with lettuce, grapefruit, and melon and is tossed in a hot-yet-sweet dressing for a salad built on contrasts of color, texture, and flavor. Serve this great summer salad chilled or at room temperature.

4	cups torn Boston or Bibb lettuce
1	large pink or red grapefruit, halved and sectioned
1	cup julienne-cut jicama
1	cup honeydew melon chunks
	Fresh mint sprigs for garnish

GRAPEFRUIT DRESSING
⅔	cup grapefruit juice, preferably fresh
½	tablespoon olive oil

1   teaspoon sugar
2   teaspoons chopped fresh mint or 1 teaspoon dried
    Pinch cayenne pepper (optional)

1. In a large mixing or serving bowl, combine lettuce with grapefruit sections, jicama, and melon.

2. Put all dressing ingredients in a jar with a tight-fitting lid. Cover and shake until thoroughly blended.

3. Spoon dressing over grapefruit-jicama mixture in bowl and toss gently to cover ingredients with dressing. Serve garnished with mint sprigs.

SERVES 4 V

PER SERVING: 100 CALORIES; 1.5 GRAMS PROTEIN; 18.7 GRAMS CARBOHYDRATES; 2.0 GRAMS FAT; 0 MILLIGRAMS CHOLESTEROL; 10 MILLIGRAMS SODIUM (WITHOUT SALTING).

PASTA and GRAINS

◆◆◆◆◆

PASTA AL ARRIBIATA

▶▶▶▶▶▶▶▶▶▶▶▶▶▶▶▶▶▶▶▶▶▶▶▶▶▶

Loosely translated from Italian, the word *arribiata* means "hot under the collar." And hot it is! Vary the heat according to your threshold for it, but the sauce is meant to be quite spicy. Be aware, the tomatoes cook very quickly on high heat to retain the slightly acid taste, so keep an eye on the skillet . . . not on the clock!

Spoon over penne or any other sturdy pasta and present it as a side dish or entrée. Accompany with a good, crusty Italian bread to sop up the sauce.

1	tablespoon olive oil
2	large cloves garlic, flattened
1	28-ounce can no-salt-added plum tomatoes in juice
¾	teaspoon hot pepper flakes or to taste
2	tablespoons dry red wine
¾	pound sturdy pasta, preferably penne
	Salt and freshly ground pepper to taste
4	large fresh basil leaves, shredded

1. Put pasta water on to boil.

2. Heat oil in a large, deep skillet or pot and sauté garlic over medium heat until lightly golden.

3. Raise heat to high and add tomatoes by the large spoonful, crushing them with the side of the spoon as you add them. When all tomatoes are added, pour in the juice left in the can. When mixture returns to a boil, let boil about 2 or 3 minutes or until liquid is slightly reduced. Reduce heat

to medium, add hot pepper flakes and wine and keep at a simmer.

    4. While tomatoes simmer, slide pasta into boiling water.

    5. When pasta is cooked to desired degree of doneness, drain and add to skillet with sauce. Stir in salt and pepper and basil, cook for 1 minute and serve.

SERVES 4 V

PER SERVING: 395 CALORIES; 13.1 GRAMS PROTEIN; 73.7 GRAMS CARBOHYDRATES; 5.5 GRAMS FAT; 0 MILLIGRAMS CHOLESTEROL; 35 MILLIGRAMS SODIUM (WITHOUT SALTING).

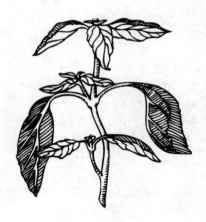

LINGUINE WITH CAULIFLOWER
AND TOASTED BREAD CRUMBS

The northern region of Italy is justly famous for its creamed sauces. This recipe is my adaptation of a noble Milanese tradition but the crisp cauliflower is stirred into a sauce that contains only about 25 percent of the fat of the classically made one.

Serve with a vegetable salad or my Many Bean Salad (page 82).

¾ cup unflavored bread crumbs, made from day-old French bread
  Vegetable oil cooking spray
1 tablespoon olive oil
2 tablespoons chopped onion
1 clove garlic, minced
1 tablespoon unbleached all-purpose flour
½ cup Vegetable Stock (page 19) or canned low sodium broth
½ pound linguine
¼ cup low fat ricotta cheese
2 tablespoons grated low fat Parmesan
½ cup evaporated skim milk
⅛ teaspoon ground nutmeg
2 tablespoons chopped fresh parsley
1½ cups sliced cauliflower florets, crisp steamed
  Salt and freshly ground pepper to taste

1. Put pasta water on to boil.
2. Sprinkle bread crumbs into a large nonstick skillet

coated with cooking spray. Toast crumbs over medium heat, shaking skillet or stirring, until crumbs are golden. Remove from heat immediately, transfer crumbs to a bowl and set aside. Wipe out skillet.

3. In the same skillet, heat olive oil and sauté onion until wilted. Add garlic and sauté for 2 minutes; do not brown. Sprinkle flour into skillet and stir until dissolved. Add broth and stir to blend. Cook over low heat for 3 minutes.

4. Meanwhile, slide pasta into boiling water.

5. Combine ricotta and Parmesan cheeses with milk, nutmeg, and parsley, beating well. Remove skillet from heat and beat in cheese mixture. Stir in cauliflower and return skillet to low heat. Taste and adjust seasonings if necessary.

6. Drain pasta and add to skillet. Toss to blend and heat through. Do not boil. Transfer mixture to individual heated bowls and top with toasted crumbs. Serve immediately.

SERVES 4

PER SERVING: 365 CALORIES; 19.2 GRAMS PROTEIN; 63.2 GRAMS CARBOHYDRATES; 5.7 GRAMS FAT; 1.7 MILLIGRAMS CHOLESTEROL; 200 MILLIGRAMS SODIUM (WITHOUT SALTING).

◆◆◆◆◆

CAPPELLINI WITH MUSHROOMS AND SUN-DRIED TOMATOES

▶▶▶▶▶▶▶▶▶▶▶▶▶▶▶▶▶▶▶▶▶▶▶▶▶

Here, the long, delicate, extremely thin pasta known as *capelli d'angelo*, cappellini or angel hair, is served with a sauce that is at once assertive but won't overwhelm.

Pair with a salad of arugula or watercress, torn romaine lettuce, red onion, and segmented or thinly sliced navel orange.

> 2 cups Rich Mushroom and Herb Stock (page 21) or
>   low sodium broth
> ¾ cup dry white wine
> 2 large shallots, thinly sliced
> 1 tablespoon olive oil
> ¼ pound white mushrooms, cleaned, trimmed, and
>   thinly sliced
> 2 tablespoons unseasoned tomato paste
> ⅛ teaspoon cayenne pepper, or to taste
> ¾ pound cappellini (angel hair pasta)
> ⅓ cup diced unseasoned sun-dried tomatoes, softened
>   in hot water and drained
>   Salt and freshly ground pepper to taste

1. Put pasta water on to boil.

2. In a medium saucepan, bring stock and wine to a boil and reduce to about 1¾ cups. Set aside.

3. In a large, deep nonstick skillet, sauté shallots in oil over low heat until soft. Add mushrooms, raise heat to medium and cook, shaking pan occasionally, until mushroom

liquid has evaporated and mushrooms are flecked with gold. Add tomato paste and cayenne and stir until well blended.

4. Slide pasta into boiling water.

5. Add reduced stock-wine mixture and sun-dried tomatoes to skillet and bring to a boil. Add salt, if desired, and generous grindings of pepper. Cook over very low heat for 5 minutes, stirring frequently.

6. Drain cooked pasta and add to skillet, tossing to coat with sauce. Serve immediately.

SERVES 4 V
PER SERVING: 395 CALORIES; 24.5 GRAMS PROTEIN; 73.0 GRAMS CARBOHYDRATES; 5.0 GRAMS FAT; 0 MILLIGRAMS CHOLESTEROL; 60 MILLIGRAMS SODIUM (WITHOUT SALTING).

◆◆◆◆◆

PASTA SHELLS
WITH BROCCOLI RABE

▶▶▶▶▶▶▶▶▶▶▶▶▶▶▶▶▶▶▶▶▶▶▶

Also called *brocoletti di rape* and *rapini*, broccoli rabe is a pungent, almost bitter-flavored green greatly favored by Italian cooks who fry, steam, or braise it. Fresh rabe can be found in markets with specialty produce sections, but if unavailable you can use kale.

The dish benefits from its brief cooking time to ensure the flavors and colors remain fresh and bright.

3 teaspoons olive oil
3 cloves garlic, pressed
4 fresh plum tomatoes, roughly chopped
¼ teaspoon hot pepper flakes, or to taste
½ pound small pasta shells, cooked al dente
1 pound broccoli rabe, cut into 1-inch pieces
   Salt and freshly ground pepper to taste

1. Heat oil in a large nonstick skillet. Add garlic, tomatoes, and hot pepper flakes. Cook over low heat, stirring, for 3 minutes.

2. Remove skillet from heat, add pasta shells and set aside.

3. Cook broccoli rabe in boiling water until tender, about 3 to 5 minutes. Drain and add to pasta shells. Toss to combine and cook briefly, until all ingredients are heated through.

SERVES 4 V

PER SERVING: 285 CALORIES; 10.1 GRAMS PROTEIN; 51.0 GRAMS CARBOHYDRATES; 4.5 GRAMS FAT; 0 MILLIGRAMS CHOLESTEROL; 35 MILLIGRAMS SODIUM (WITHOUT SALTING).

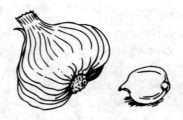

◆◆◆◆◆

LINGUINE
WITH ZUCCHINI AND ALMONDS

▶▶▶▶▶▶▶▶▶▶▶▶▶▶▶▶▶▶▶▶▶▶▶

In the world of nuts, almonds have one of the best ratios of nutrients to calories and are a source of protein, calcium, riboflavin, and vitamin E. Although relatively high in fat, it is primarily a monounsaturated fat. Here the almonds add crunch to this quickly prepared recipe.

> 2   teaspoons olive oil
> 2   cups diced zucchini
> 1   small onion, chopped
> 1   clove garlic, pressed
> 1   cup canned no-salt-added tomato sauce
> ¼   teaspoon dried oregano
> ¼   teaspoon red pepper flakes (optional)
> ¼   teaspoon dried rosemary
> ½   teaspoon sugar
>   Salt and freshly ground pepper to taste
> ½   pound linguine, cooked al dente
> ¼   cup toasted, slivered, and blanched almonds

1. Heat olive oil in a nonstick skillet. Add zucchini, onion, and garlic. Cook until zucchini is just tender.

2. Add tomato sauce and all seasonings. Bring sauce to a simmer and cook, stirring occasionally, for about 10 minutes or until all ingredients are hot and thoroughly combined.

3. Spoon zucchini mixture over linguine, top with almonds, and serve.

SERVES 4 V

PER SERVING: 305 CALORIES; 10.3 GRAMS PROTEIN; 51.5 GRAMS CARBOHYDRATES; 6.7 GRAMS FAT; 0 MILLIGRAMS CHOLESTEROL; 20 MILLIGRAMS SODIUM (WITHOUT SALTING).

◆ ◆ ◆ ◆ ◆

PASTA BOWS
WITH SWEET AND SOUR CABBAGE

▶ ▶

In my version the sweet and sour cabbage is made with hot paprika and a seedless orange for an offsetting and different taste. Bow-tie pasta or farfalle, more frequently found combined with kasha, is used here.

Serve this unique and hearty entrée with pumpernickel.

½	cup Vegetable Stock (page 19) or canned low sodium broth
1	medium onion, diced
1	medium head cabbage, cored and shredded
2	teaspoons dark brown sugar
⅛	teaspoon hot paprika or to taste
¼	teaspoon freshly ground pepper
1	seedless orange, separated into segments
½	pound small pasta bows, cooked al dente
	Salt to taste

1. In a large pot combine stock, onion, cabbage, sugar, paprika, and ground pepper. Cover, and cook over low heat, stirring occasionally, for about 15 minutes or until cabbage is wilted.

2. Add orange, pasta, and salt if desired, to cabbage and toss gently to blend ingredients. Cook briefly over low heat, uncovered, until ingredients are heated through.

SERVES 4 V

PER SERVING: 285 CALORIES; 10.3 GRAMS PROTEIN; 59.3 GRAMS CARBOHYDRATES; 1.3 GRAMS FAT; 0 MILLIGRAMS CHOLESTEROL; 55 MILLIGRAMS SODIUM (WITHOUT SALTING).

◆ ◆ ◆ ◆ ◆

TOASTED EGG BARLEY
WITH SCALLIONS AND RADISH

▶ ▶

J ust as orzo is a tiny rice-shaped pasta, egg barley is also a pasta product but cut into the shape of barley. Both are wonderful in soups and can be used as an alternative to rice or other small pasta. Because most people are unfamiliar with it, there's lots of guessing going on at the table until the cook reveals it's another form of pasta.

Egg barley comes in half-pound packages and is sold toasted and plain. If the toasted is not available, the plain may be used just as successfully, but the toasted has a darker color and cooks up just a bit more *al dente*. If neither is available at your market, substitute orzo, pastina, or other tiny pasta.

2	teaspoons vegetable oil
½	pound toasted egg barley
6	scallions, white parts and tender greens, finely chopped
⅛	teaspoon ground chili pepper
1½	cups Vegetable Stock (page 19) or canned low sodium broth
	Salt to taste
2	cups sliced red radish

1. Heat vegetable oil in a large nonstick skillet. Add toasted egg barley and cook over medium heat, stirring, for 1 minute.

2. Add scallions, chili pepper, and stock to skillet. Stir to

combine. Reduce heat, cover, and cook over low heat for about 15 minutes, or until liquid is absorbed and egg barley is tender. If egg barley is not cooked *al dente* at this point, add an additional 2 tablespoons of water.

3. Add salt, if desired, and stir in sliced radish before serving.

SERVES 4 V

PER SERVING: 260 CALORIES; 8.7 GRAMS PROTEIN; 34.5 GRAMS CARBOHYDRATES; 5.8 GRAMS FAT; 0 MILLIGRAMS CHOLESTEROL; 55 MILLIGRAMS SODIUM (WITHOUT SALTING).

◆ ◆ ◆ ◆ ◆

RED PEPPER RISOTTO
WITH FRESH CORN

▶ ▶

Ideal for the patient home cook, this festive dish has the aura of sophistication that belies its healthful benefits. The outstanding flavor of this dish is best accompanied by a low-key, simple salad—perhaps chilled Bibb lettuce with subtle Lemon Vinaigrette (page 85).

4½   cups Vegetable Stock (page 19) or canned low
       sodium broth, approximately
¾   cup dry white wine
½   pound Arborio rice
1   small onion, chopped
1   clove garlic, minced
1½   tablespoons olive oil
¾   cup finely diced red bell pepper
4   pitted black olives, thinly sliced
1¼   cup fresh corn kernels, or frozen and thawed
1   tablespoon chopped fresh basil or ½ tablespoon
       dried
       Salt and freshly ground pepper to taste
4   tablespoons low fat Parmesan cheese (optional)

1. Combine stock and wine in a saucepan, heat to simmering and keep at a simmer.

2. Sauté rice, onion, and garlic in oil for 2 minutes or until rice begins to brown and onion is tender.

3. Pour in a ladleful of stock and cook, stirring, until liquid is absorbed. Promptly add another ladleful of stock

---

and repeat procedure. Continue until stock is nearly used up and rice is creamy.

4. Add red pepper, olives, corn, and basil to rice mixture and continue to stir until ingredients are heated through and rice is very creamy.

5. Taste and adjust seasonings. Pass Parmesan separately, if desired.

SERVES 4 V

PER SERVING: 370 CALORIES; 10.0 GRAMS PROTEIN; 68.0 GRAMS CARBOHYDRATES; 7.3 GRAMS FAT; 2.8 MILLIGRAMS CHOLESTEROL; 180 MILLIGRAMS SODIUM (WITHOUT SALTING).

◆ ◆ ◆ ◆ ◆

RISOTTO WITH MUSHROOMS, SHALLOTS, PEAS, AND FONTINA

▶ ▶

This recipe is an updated variation of a classic dish made with prosciutto, heaps of heavy cream, lots of butter, mushrooms, and peas. In this *Good Eating* version, the ham, butter, and cream go and we greet, instead, a tasty mélange of mushrooms, tiny green peas, Fontina cheese, and shallots.

On the side, present a bowl of lightly steamed string beans with diced pimientos sprinkled with fresh dill weed.

5	cups Rich Mushroom and Herb Stock (page 21) or 3 cups stock and 3 cups water, approximately
1	tablespoon olive oil
2	large shallots, thinly sliced
1	small clove garlic, chopped
4	ounces fresh white mushrooms, cleaned and sliced
½	pound Arborio rice
1½	cups tiny green peas, fresh or frozen and thawed
1	ounce Fontina cheese, finely diced
	Salt and coarsely ground pepper to taste

1. Heat broth to simmering in a medium saucepan and keep hot.

2. Sauté shallots and garlic in oil for 2 minutes, then add mushrooms and cook over medium heat until liquid is evaporated and mushrooms are tender. Add rice and cook for 2 minutes or until grains are coated with shallot-mushroom mixture.

3. Pour in a ladleful of broth and cook, stirring, until

liquid is absorbed. Promptly add another ladleful of stock and repeat procedure. Continue until stock is nearly used up and rice is almost creamy.

4. Stir in peas and Fontina and cook, stirring, until cheese begins to melt. Add salt, if desired, and generous grindings of pepper. Serve hot.

SERVES 4

PER SERVING: 335 CALORIES; 9.3 GRAMS PROTEIN; 58.1 GRAMS CARBOHYDRATES; 6.2 GRAMS FAT; 6.2 MILLIGRAMS CHOLESTEROL; 75 MILLIGRAMS SODIUM (WITHOUT SALTING).

◆ ◆ ◆ ◆ ◆

BULGUR PILAF

▶ ▶

Contrary to the myth, bulgur is not cracked wheat! Cracked wheat is uncooked wheat that has been dried first and cracked apart later by coarse milling. Bulgur, on the other hand, is wheat that has been steamed, then dried before being crushed into various grinds. And because bulgur is only minimally processed, it retains its high vitamin content.

2	teaspoons vegetable oil
1	medium onion, chopped
1	cup thinly sliced white mushrooms
1	medium green bell pepper, seeded and chopped
1	tablespoon chopped parsley
1	cup bulgur
¼	teaspoon ground cumin or to taste
	Salt and freshly ground pepper to taste
2	cups Vegetable Stock (page 19) or canned low sodium broth

1. Heat oil in a large nonstick skillet. Add onion, mushrooms, and green pepper, and cook, stirring, for 3 to 5 minutes or until onion is translucent.

2. Add parsley and bulgur to skillet, and continue cooking, stirring, until bulgur is golden.

3. Add seasonings and stock. Cover and bring to a boil. Reduce heat to low, and simmer gently for 15 to 20 minutes,

---

or until bulgur is tender and liquid is absorbed. Serve immediately.

SERVES 4 V

PER SERVING: 170 CALORIES; 5.3 GRAMS PROTEIN; 32.7 GRAMS CARBOHYDRATES; 3.1 GRAMS FAT; 0 MILLIGRAMS CHOLESTEROL; 40 MILLIGRAMS SODIUM (WITHOUT SALTING).

◆ ◆ ◆ ◆ ◆

COUSCOUS
WITH TOMATOES AND SCALLIONS

▶ ▶

Couscous, a semolina-like cereal, is a favorite in some Middle Eastern countries. In Morocco it is frequently referred to as their National Dish, and is often combined with meats as well as vegetables. This version is very low in fat, cooks quickly, and also makes an excellent light lunch (try it chilled) for six or a side dish for eight.

>   4   ripe fresh plum tomatoes, roughly chopped
>   4   scallions, with tops, roughly chopped
>   1½   tablespoons balsamic vinegar or to taste
>   ¼   teaspoon freshly ground pepper to taste
>   3   cups Vegetable Stock (page 19) or canned low
>   sodium broth
>   2   cups couscous
>   Salt to taste
>   2   tablespoons finely chopped fresh basil or parsley

1. Combine tomatoes and scallions in a bowl. Add vinegar and pepper, toss lightly to combine ingredients, and set aside.

2. Bring stock to a rolling boil in a large saucepan. Stir in couscous, cover, and remove from heat. Let stand, covered, for 5 to 7 minutes or until liquid is absorbed.

3. Fluff couscous with a fork. Transfer to a serving bowl and stir in tomato mixture, adding salt, if desired. Taste and adjust seasonings if necessary. Sprinkle with chopped basil and serve warm or chilled.

SERVES 4 V

PER SERVING: 385 CALORIES; 13.0 GRAMS PROTEIN; 79.5
GRAMS CARBOHYDRATES; 1.2 GRAMS FAT; 0 MILLIGRAMS
CHOLESTEROL; 65 MILLIGRAMS SODIUM (WITHOUT SALTING).

◆ ◆ ◆ ◆ ◆

POLENTA WITH MUSHROOMS

▶ ▶

Polenta, a northern Italian favorite, may be prepared in advance, chilled, and sliced—then grilled or broiled. Polenta makes an excellent base, and may be served with a bit of low fat grated cheese, a pasta sauce, or grilled fresh vegetables.

½   *pound mushrooms, thinly sliced*
1   *large clove garlic, pressed*
½   *cup Vegetable Stock (page 19) or canned low
      sodium broth
      Salt and freshly ground pepper to taste*
6   *cups water*
1½ *cups coarse yellow cornmeal*
1½ *tablespoons chopped fresh parsley*

1. Combine mushrooms, garlic, and stock in saucepan. Cover, and cook over low heat until mushrooms are tender, about 10 minutes. Season to taste and reserve.

2. Heat water in a large saucepan. When water comes to a boil turn heat down so that water is just simmering. Add cornmeal in a thin stream, stirring with a wooden spoon.

3. Continue stirring after all the cornmeal has been added. Cook for about 20 minutes, or until polenta pulls away from the sides of the saucepan as you stir.

4. Spoon the polenta onto a platter and pour mushrooms and liquid over polenta. Garnish with parsley and serve immediately.

SERVES 4 V

PER SERVING: 200 CALORIES; 4.9 GRAMS PROTEIN; 41.7 GRAMS CARBOHYDRATES; 1.0 GRAMS FAT; 0 MILLIGRAMS CHOLESTEROL; 15 MILLIGRAMS SODIUM (WITHOUT SALTING).

ENTRÉES

◆ ◆ ◆ ◆

CABBAGE ROLLS WITH RAISINS AND SUNFLOWER SEEDS

▶ ▶

In a recipe with so many diverse elements, it's important to have all the ingredients assembled. The filling, which contains brown rice, raisins, seeds, and spices, is spooned into blanched cabbage leaves, then gently simmered in a delicious sauce until completely cooked.

Serve with crisp-steamed fresh green beans or peas dotted with pearl onions.

1	large head cabbage
2	teaspoons vegetable oil
1	medium onion, grated
1	cup brown rice
2	cups Vegetable Stock (page 19) or canned low sodium broth
3	tablespoons raisins
¼	cup toasted sunflower seeds
½	teaspoon ground cumin
¼	teaspoon ground cardamom
	Salt and freshly ground pepper to taste
3	cups canned no-salt-added tomato sauce
1	cup water
1	teaspoon sugar

1. Parboil cabbage in boiling water for 10 to 15 minutes, or until cabbage is almost tender. Drain and set aside to cool.
2. Heat oil in a nonstick skillet. Sauté onion in skillet,

stirring, for 2 minutes. Add rice, and sauté for an additional 2 minutes.

3. Add vegetable stock or broth, raisins, sunflower seeds, and seasonings. Bring to a simmer, cover, and cook for 30 minutes.

4. Separate cabbage into individual leaves. Spoon two tablespoons of rice mixture on each leaf. Roll, carefully tucking in sides of each leaf after first roll. Place cabbage rolls in a Dutch oven or large casserole and set aside.

5. Combine tomato sauce, water, and sugar in a saucepan and bring to a simmer. Let sauce simmer gently for 2 minutes, stirring frequently.

6. Pour sauce over cabbage rolls, cover, and simmer over low heat for 45 minutes to 1 hour or until cabbage and rice are completely cooked.

SERVES 6 V

PER SERVING: 275 CALORIES; 7.4 GRAMS PROTEIN; 49.2 GRAMS CARBOHYDRATES; 6.2 GRAMS FAT; 0 MILLIGRAMS CHOLESTEROL; 115 MILLIGRAMS SODIUM (WITHOUT SALTING).

◆ ◆ ◆ ◆ ◆

PEPPERS STUFFED WITH BEANS AND RICE

▶ ▶

This recipe is a favorite in my household. Easy to prepare, satisfying, and impressive to behold. After assembling the ingredients, you need only stuff the peppers' cavities, pour in the stock, and your stove will do the rest of the work.

A real people-pleaser, this amalgam of rice-beans-peppers is a highly nutritious and savory dish. Serve with Harvard or steamed beets and, of course, good crusty bread.

4   *medium green bell peppers*
1   *cup cooked white beans, or canned (no-salt-added or well-rinsed), puréed*
1½ *cups cooked brown or white rice*
1   *medium tomato, finely chopped*
1   *tablespoon vegetable oil*
1   *medium onion, grated*
2   *tablespoons chopped fresh parsley*
    Salt and freshly ground pepper to taste
2   *cups Vegetable Stock (page 19) or canned low sodium broth*

1. Carefully cut tops off green peppers and remove seeds. Reserve peppers and tops.
2. Combine all remaining ingredients, except stock or broth, mix thoroughly, and stuff mixture into peppers. Cover peppers with their tops and place in a Dutch oven or casserole.

3. Pour vegetable stock or broth around peppers, and, if necessary, add enough water so that peppers are half covered. Cover and simmer over very low heat for about 1 hour, or until peppers are tender, adding additional water if too much liquid evaporates.

4. Remove peppers from Dutch oven and place on a platter. Serve hot or cover loosely, refrigerate, and serve chilled.

SERVES 4 V

PER SERVING: 225 CALORIES; 7.3 GRAMS PROTEIN; 39.2 GRAMS CARBOHYDRATES; 4.1 GRAMS FAT; 0 MILLIGRAMS CHOLESTEROL; 45 MILLIGRAMS SODIUM (WITHOUT SALTING).

◆ ◆ ◆ ◆

CURRIED EGGPLANT, ZUCCHINI, AND CHICK-PEA STEW

▶ ▶

Commercial curry powder generally comes in two degrees of heat: standard, which is mild, and *Madras*, which is hot. You may wish to amplify or modify its sizzle. This is accomplished with surprising ease. For a hit of Hades add cayenne, red or black peppers, or chilies to the mix. For a tamer blend, skip the hot pepper flakes and add a little cinnamon, cloves, and/or the rind from a lemon, lime, or orange.

Pita bread or basmati rice are natural partners of any curry, as are raita and chutney.

2	cups Vegetable Stock (*page 19*) or canned low sodium broth
2	tablespoons curry powder
¼	teaspoon hot pepper flakes (*optional*)
4–6	small eggplants (*about 2 pounds total*), ends trimmed and cubed
4	small zucchini, sliced
2	cups chopped coarsely diced tomatoes, fresh or canned (*no-salt-added*)
2	cups cooked chick-peas, or canned (*no-salt-added or well-rinsed and drained*)

1. Heat stock in a Dutch oven or stove-top casserole. Stir in curry powder and hot pepper flakes, if desired, and bring to a simmer.

2. Add eggplant and let simmer over low heat for 5

minutes. Add zucchini and tomatoes and cook for an additional 3 to 5 minutes, or until zucchini is barely tender.

3. Add chick-peas, and continue to simmer for 5 to 10 minutes, or until eggplant is cooked and all ingredients are heated through.

SERVES 4 V

PER SERVING: 245 CALORIES; 12.0 GRAMS PROTEIN; 47.3 GRAMS CARBOHYDRATES; 3.7 GRAMS FAT; 0 MILLIGRAMS CHOLESTEROL; 60 MILLIGRAMS SODIUM (WITHOUT SALTING).

◆ ◆ ◆ ◆
VEGETABLE-RICE CAKES
WITH TOMATO AND ONION RELISH
▶ ▶

In this recipe the combination of vegetables, brown rice, and cornmeal makes a delicious and filling cake. In addition, the bold and chunky uncooked tomato-onion-cilantro relish can also be used as a topping for meatless burgers, in tacos and tortillas, scrambled with tofu, or with sliced avocados as a kind of composed guacamole. A dash of hot pepper would add a friendly jolt.

2	teaspoons olive oil
1	medium onion, chopped
1	clove garlic, minced
1	small red bell pepper, diced
1	small stalk celery, diced
5	ounces fresh spinach, trimmed, well rinsed, drained, and shredded
1	cup corn kernels, fresh or frozen and thawed
2	tablespoons minced fresh parsley or 1 tablespoon dried
	Salt and freshly ground pepper to taste
1	cup cooked brown rice
½	cup self-rising cornmeal
	Egg substitute equal to 2 eggs, or 1 large egg and 1 egg white
	Vegetable oil cooking spray

TOMATO AND ONION RELISH
2	just-ripe plum tomatoes, diced

½   medium red onion, minced
3   tablespoons red wine vinegar
2   tablespoons minced fresh cilantro or parsley
2   teaspoons olive oil

1. Heat oil in a nonstick skillet. Add onions, garlic, red pepper, and celery and cook over medium heat for 5 minutes, stirring frequently.

2. Add spinach, corn, parsley, and seasonings to skillet. Cook 2 minutes, then reduce heat, cover and cook an additional 5 minutes, stirring often. Remove from heat, cover, and let stand about 2 minutes.

3. Transfer ingredients from skillet into a mixing bowl and let cool slightly.

4. Add rice, cornmeal, and egg substitute to vegetables in bowl and mix until ingredients are thoroughly blended. Shape mixture into 8 cakes (if mixture is too dry to shape, add a little water or broth; if too moist add a little more cornmeal).

5. Spray a large, nonstick skillet lightly with cooking oil and heat. Add cakes to skillet and cook until golden brown on both sides.

6. While cakes cook, prepare relish by blending together all relish ingredients. When cakes are browned, transfer to a platter or serving dishes. Serve relish separately or spoon over cakes.

SERVES 4

PER SERVING: 240 CALORIES; 8.2 GRAMS PROTEIN; 37.0 GRAMS CARBOHYDRATES; 6.7 GRAMS FAT; 0 MILLIGRAMS CHOLESTEROL; 300 MILLIGRAMS SODIUM (WITHOUT SALTING).

BULGUR-STUFFED EGGPLANT

▶ ▶

𝕐 ou've probably eaten bulgur as the prime ingredient in that delicious Middle Eastern dish called *tabbouleh*. But you may be unfamiliar with these nutritious wheat kernels that have been steamed, dried, and crushed. Bulgur has a tender, chewy texture and comes in coarse, medium, and fine grades, and is excellent in pilaf, salads, and in vegetable dishes such as this.

Serve with raita and a basket of crisp breads such as lavosh, matzos, or pita chips.

2	eggplants (*about 1 pound each*)
2	cups bulgur
2	cups Vegetable Stock (*page 19*) *or canned low sodium broth*
2	cups water
2	teaspoons olive oil
1	small onion, minced
1	small tomato, finely chopped
1	tablespoon balsamic vinegar
	Salt and freshly ground pepper to taste
1	tablespoon finely chopped fresh mint or ½ tablespoon dried

1. Preheat oven to 350° F.

2. Pierce each eggplant in 2 or 3 places. Place eggplant on a flat, nonstick baking pan and bake for 20 to 30 minutes, turning twice, until eggplant is tender.

3. While eggplant is baking, combine bulgur, broth, and

water in a large saucepan. Cover and bring to a boil. Reduce heat and let simmer gently for 15 to 20 minutes, or until bulgur is tender and liquid is absorbed.

4. When eggplant is baked, remove from oven and let cool. Carefully cut each eggplant in half, scoop out eggplant pulp and chop coarsely, reserving shells.

5. Place chopped eggplant in a bowl. Add bulgur, olive oil, onion, tomato, vinegar, and seasonings, and mix to combine.

6. Spoon eggplant-bulgur mixture into eggplant shells, smoothing top with back of spoon, garnish with chopped mint and serve.

SERVES 4 V

PER SERVING: 380 CALORIES; 12.3 GRAMS PROTEIN; 78.2 GRAMS CARBOHYDRATES; 6.1 GRAMS FAT; 0 MILLIGRAMS CHOLESTEROL; 55 MILLIGRAMS SODIUM (WITHOUT SALTING).

♦♦♦♦♦

MÉLANGE
OF BAKED SQUASH

►►►►►►►►►►►►►►►►►►►►►►►►►

Looking for a main course that's high in flavor but low in calories, saturated fat, and sodium? Well, your search may be over because this savory dish fits every bill.

Serve this colorful mélange with polenta, parsleyed brown or white rice, or with baked sweet potatoes or yams.

4	*medium yellow squash, sliced*
4	*medium zucchini, sliced*
1	*large red onion, chopped*
1	*clove garlic, pressed*
¼	*cup Vegetable Stock (page 19) or canned low sodium broth*
1	*tablespoon raspberry or balsamic vinegar*
1	*tablespoon olive oil*
¼	*teaspoon dried oregano*
	Salt and freshly ground pepper to taste

1. Preheat oven to 350° F.

2. Combine yellow squash, zucchini, onion, and garlic in a bowl. Mix well. Transfer to a baking dish.

3. In a separate bowl, combine stock or broth, vinegar, olive oil, and seasonings and mix until thoroughly blended. Pour over squash mixture.

4. Bake squash for 25 to 35 minutes, or until vegetables are just tender. Serve hot or at room temperature.

SERVES 4 V

PER SERVING: 100 CALORIES; 3.8 GRAMS PROTEIN; 13.4
GRAMS CARBOHYDRATES; 3.9 GRAMS FAT; 0 MILLIGRAMS
CHOLESTEROL; 15 MILLIGRAMS SODIUM (WITHOUT SALTING).

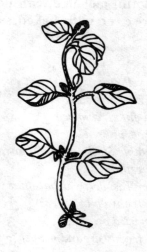

◆ ◆ ◆ ◆

VEGETABLES CHINESE STYLE

▸▸▸▸▸▸▸▸▸▸▸▸▸▸▸▸▸▸▸▸▸▸▸▸▸▸▸

Good over Oriental noodles or rice.

½   tablespoon vegetable oil
2   stalks broccoli, trimmed and cut into florets
½   head small cauliflower, trimmed and cut into
    florets
6   scallions, white and tender greens, cut into 1-inch
    pieces
1   medium green bell pepper, sliced
¼   pound white mushrooms, sliced
¾   cup canned water chestnuts, drained and rinsed
¼   cup water
2   teaspoons low sodium soy sauce
½   cup pineapple juice
1   teaspoon sesame oil

1. Heat vegetable oil in a nonstick wok or skillet. Add all vegetables and stir-fry for 2 minutes. Add water to skillet, cover, and cook vegetables until they are crisp-tender.

2. Add soy sauce, pineapple juice, and sesame oil to skillet and stir until all ingredients are combined. Serve hot.

SERVES 4 V

PER SERVING: 105 CALORIES; 4.3 GRAMS PROTEIN; 16.5 GRAMS CARBOHYDRATES; 3.1 GRAMS FAT; 0 MILLIGRAMS CHOLESTEROL; 130 MILLIGRAMS SODIUM (WITHOUT SALT-ING).

ROAST SWEET POTATOES
AND TURNIPS WITH APPLES

▶▶▶▶▶▶▶▶▶▶▶▶▶▶▶▶▶▶▶▶▶▶▶▶▶

Cardamom, which is a distinguishing ingredient in this recipe, is an aromatic spice native to India and grown in Asia, South America, and some Pacific Islands. Widely used in East Indian cooking, cardamom has a pungent aroma and imparts a warm, spicy-sweet flavor. It's delicious in stews and curries, but be forewarned: a little goes a long, flavorful way. When used with the other seasonings, vegetables, and fruit in this recipe, cardamom lends its own distinctive note to the results.

6   medium sweet potatoes, thickly sliced
4   small turnips, thinly sliced
1   medium onion, thinly sliced
1   cup apple juice
1   teaspoon ground cardamom
¼   teaspoon ground turmeric
     Salt and freshly ground pepper to taste
4   Granny Smith apples, cored, each cut into 8
     wedges

1. Preheat oven to 375° F.

2. Combine sweet potatoes, turnips, and onion in a nonstick baking pan. Add apple juice and seasonings and toss to mix.

3. Roast vegetables for 20 to 30 minutes, or until potatoes and turnips are almost tender. Add apples to pan, and

continue roasting until ingredients are brown, crusty, and tender.

SERVES 4 V

PER SERVING: 375 CALORIES; 5.6 GRAMS PROTEIN; 88.8 GRAMS CARBOHYDRATES; 1.4 GRAMS FAT; 0 MILLIGRAMS CHOLESTEROL; 125 MILLIGRAMS SODIUM (WITHOUT SALTING).

♦♦♦♦♦
LENTIL AND SPINACH GRATIN

▶▶▶▶▶▶▶▶▶▶▶▶▶▶▶▶▶▶▶▶▶▶▶▶

How can anything this nutritious taste so good? Easy. Especially when you carbo-load with calcium and vitamin A- and B-laden lentils and vitamin A- and C-rich spinach. Both are pumped with iron, contain virtually no fat, and are noted roughage dealers.

Here, the classic spice combination of ground coriander and cumin unite with other herbs and seasonings, bread crumbs, and fragrant olive oil to produce a delightful main course that's hard to resist. Serve with saffron rice or basmati rice pilaf and steaming hot paratha or other East Indian bread.

1	cup lentils, cooked
2	10-ounce bags fresh spinach, trimmed, rinsed, cooked, and chopped
½	teaspoon ground coriander
½	teaspoon ground cumin
2	tablespoons minced parsley
	Salt and freshly ground pepper to taste
½	cup bread crumbs, made from 1 slice dried whole wheat bread
2	teaspoons olive oil

1. Preheat oven to 350° F.

2. Combine lentils, spinach, coriander, cumin, parsley, salt and pepper in a bowl. Mix until combined.

3. Spoon lentil-spinach mixture into a baking dish. Sprinkle bread crumbs on top and drizzle olive oil over

crumbs. Bake for 15 to 20 minutes or until a light brown crust has formed and all ingredients are hot. Serve immediately.

SERVES 4 V

PER SERVING: 120 CALORIES; 7.9 GRAMS PROTEIN; 16.5 GRAMS CARBOHYDRATES; 3.1 GRAMS FAT; 0 MILLIGRAMS CHOLESTEROL; 120 MILLIGRAMS SODIUM (WITHOUT SALTING).

BOMBAY CURRY

▶ ▶

In this recipe I have suggested side orders of peanuts, raisins, and scallions, but you might also add plain steamed rice, cucumbers and tomatoes, and a chutney or two (see Gingered Peach and Pepper Chutney, page 13, and Plum Almond Chutney, page 15).

½	pound potatoes, peeled, cut into ½-inch cubes and cooked
¼	pound green beans, cut into 2-inch lengths, and cooked
2	medium carrots, cut into 1-inch lengths, and cooked
1	cup low fat plain yogurt
1	teaspoon all-purpose flour
1	teaspoon curry powder
½	teaspoon ground coriander
½	teaspoon ground cumin
2	tablespoons shelled, chopped, unsalted peanuts
¼	cup raisins
3	scallions, chopped

1. Combine potatoes, green beans, and carrots in a saucepan and reserve.

2. Place yogurt in a bowl, add flour, and stir for 1 minute. Add curry powder, coriander, and cumin and mix until all ingredients are blended.

3. Pour yogurt mixture over vegetables in saucepan

and allow all ingredients to heat through over low heat, stirring often. Do not let mixture come to a boil.

4. Spoon curried vegetables into a serving bowl, and present peanuts, raisins, and scallions in individual bowls on the side.

SERVES 4

PER SERVING: 170 CALORIES; 6.8 GRAMS PROTEIN; 30.0 GRAMS CARBOHYDRATES; 3.5 GRAMS FAT; 3.5 MILLIGRAMS CHOLESTEROL; 65 MILLIGRAMS SODIUM (WITHOUT SALTING).

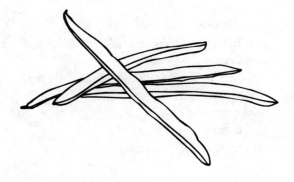

◆ ◆ ◆ ◆ ◆

ARTICHOKES
STUFFED WITH CHILI-CORN

▶ ▶

After creating a welcoming nest in the center of the artichoke by gently spreading its leaves, it's easy to mound the flavorful chili-corn within. While pleasing friends and family with this unusual and attractive dish, you can also boast about its ample supply of potassium, vitamins A and C, and fiber.

Serve with a basket of hot baked taco chips, shredded lettuce with sliced tomatoes, and guacamole (made with a higher than usual ratio of tomato and onions to the avocado).

2   teaspoons vegetable oil
1   small green bell pepper, seeded and chopped
1   small onion, chopped
1   10-ounce package frozen whole kernel corn,
    thawed and drained
1   tablespoon hot or mild chili powder or to taste
    Salt to taste
4   large artichokes, cooked and kept warm

1. Heat oil in a nonstick skillet. Add green pepper and onion, and cook over medium-low heat until pepper and onion are translucent. Stir in corn, chili, and salt. Reduce heat to very low and let simmer about 3 minutes or until heated through.

2. Gently pull open center leaves of each artichoke, removing some of the center leaves and the choke, creating a

space to hold corn filling. Spoon hot corn mixture into each artichoke and serve.

SERVES 4 V

PER SERVING: 175 CALORIES; 7.8 GRAMS PROTEIN; 34.7 GRAMS CARBOHYDRATES; 3.4 GRAMS FAT; 0 MILLIGRAMS CHOLESTEROL; 165 MILLIGRAMS SODIUM (WITHOUT SALTING).

BLACK-EYED PEA CHILI
WITH TOFU

▶ ▶

Blocks of tofu deliver a "meaty" quality and provide protein, calcium, and B vitamins to vegetarian diets. This "chili con tofu" made with black-eyeds is no exception. Don't be turned off by the number of ingredients listed because this one-dish meal, with its unique consistency and aroma, is sure to turn you on.

2	teaspoons vegetable oil
2	medium onions, diced
3	cloves garlic, minced
2	stalks celery, diced
1	medium green bell pepper, trimmed and diced
1	medium red bell pepper, trimmed and diced
1	6-ounce can unseasoned tomato paste
3	cups water
¾	cup dry red wine
2	cups black-eyed peas, soaked overnight, rinsed and drained
2	medium carrots, diced
4	ripe plum tomatoes, diced, with its juice
2	tablespoons chili powder or to taste
2	tablespoons minced fresh parsley or 1 tablespoon dried
1	teaspoon dried coriander
½	teaspoon ground cinnamon
¼	teaspoon cayenne pepper or to taste

8   ounces firm tofu, drained and cut into ¾-inch
     cubes
     Salt and freshly ground pepper to taste

1. Heat oil in a large stock pot. Add onion, garlic, celery, and green and red peppers, stirring over medium-low heat for 5 minutes or until vegetables are tender.

2. Stir in tomato paste, water, and wine. Raise heat to high and bring to a boil. Reduce heat to low, add all remaining ingredients, except tofu and salt and pepper. Stir well to blend, cover, and let simmer gently for 2 hours, stirring occasionally and adding additional water if too much liquid evaporates.

3. Add tofu and continue to cook for an additional 30 minutes, or until peas are tender. Taste, adjust seasonings and add salt and pepper, if desired.

SERVES 6 V
PER SERVING: 175 CALORIES; 7.2 GRAMS PROTEIN; 28.5 GRAMS CARBOHYDRATES; 4.4 GRAMS FAT; 0 MILLIGRAMS CHOLESTEROL; 80 MILLIGRAMS SODIUM (WITHOUT SALTING).

TOFU SHEPHERD'S PIE
(Adapted from Kelly Sinclair)

▶ ▶

The tofu-walnuts-peas troika is a sturdy vegetarian stand-in for the ground lamb or mutton of the original. The marvelous spices used in this version are as savory as they are exotic. Classically, it is mixed with gravy and crowned with mashed potatoes, then baked until the potato "crust" browns, producing a homey, filling, enjoyable plate.

12	ounces medium-firm tofu, frozen at least 24 hours and thawed
2	teaspoons vegetable oil
1	large onion, chopped
3	tablespoons chopped toasted walnuts
½	teaspoon ground coriander
¼	teaspoon dried thyme
¼	teaspoon freshly ground black pepper
½	cup frozen and thawed green peas
	Juice of ½ large lemon
2	teaspoons low sodium tamari soy sauce
4	large potatoes, peeled and cubed
¾	cup soy milk or low fat milk
	Salt to taste (optional)
	Vegetable oil cooking spray

MUSHROOM GRAVY

2	teaspoons vegetable oil
½	pound white mushrooms, trimmed, wiped clean, and sliced

1   tablespoon low sodium soy sauce
    Salt and freshly ground black pepper to taste
1½ cups hot potato cooking water
2   tablespoons cornstarch dissolved in ½ cup
    water

1. Drain tofu well, squeezing out as much moisture as possible, shred and set aside.

2. Heat oil in a large, nonstick skillet. Add onion and cook until translucent. Stir in walnuts, coriander, thyme, pepper, and tofu. Cook over medium heat, stirring, for about 2 minutes or until ingredients are thoroughly heated. Stir in green peas, lemon juice, and tamari. Cover, remove from heat and set aside.

3. Preheat oven to 350° F.

4. Boil potatoes until tender. Drain potatoes and reserve 1½ cups of the cooking water. Mash potatoes with milk and salt, if desired.

5. To make gravy, heat oil, stir in mushrooms, soy sauce, and pepper. Cook over medium-low heat until mushrooms are tender, stirring occasionally. Add potato water and bring to a boil. Slowly stir in cornstarch mixture and cook at a low boil, continuing to stir, until gravy is clear and thickened.

6. Spread tofu mixture over bottom of nonstick baking pan. Spoon gravy over tofu and cover with a layer of mashed potatoes. Lightly coat surface of potatoes with cooking spray and bake for 15 to 20 minutes or until top is golden.

SERVES 4 V

PER SERVING: 330 CALORIES; 15.3 GRAMS PROTEIN; 44.8 GRAMS CARBOHYDRATES; 11.1 GRAMS FAT; 0 MILLIGRAMS CHOLESTEROL; 295 MILLIGRAMS SODIUM (WITHOUT SALTING).

◆ ◆ ◆ ◆

POTATOES, PEAS, AND LENTILS IN SPICED TOMATO SAUCE

▶ ▶

A salad of crisp seasonal greens tossed with fresh lemon juice and a dash of olive oil is an ideal accompaniment to this one-dish meal.

4	*large potatoes, peeled, cooked, and cubed*
2	*cups cooked lentils*
2	*teaspoons olive oil*
1	*large onion, diced*
2	*cloves garlic, minced*
1	*cup petite green peas, fresh or frozen and thawed*
2	*cups canned no-salt-added tomato sauce*
½	*teaspoon ground coriander*
¼	*teaspoon ground cumin*
¼	*teaspoon ground ginger*
¼	*teaspoon hot pepper flakes or to taste*
	Salt to taste

1. Combine potatoes and lentils in a bowl and set aside.

2. Heat oil in a large, nonstick skillet. Add onion and garlic and cook, stirring, for 2 minutes.

3. Add peas, tomato sauce, and seasonings to skillet and continue cooking until sauce simmers. Stir reserved vegetables into sauce. Cover and cook until all ingredients are hot.

SERVES 4 V

PER SERVING: 325 CALORIES; 15.3 GRAMS PROTEIN; 59.0 GRAMS CARBOHYDRATES; 3.1 GRAMS FAT; 0 MILLIGRAMS CHOLESTEROL; 50 MILLIGRAMS SODIUM (WITHOUT SALTING).

◆ ◆ ◆ ◆ ◆

OKRA WITH CORN, TOMATOES, AND HOT PEPPER SAUCE

▶ ▶

Whenever I prepare this dish I think about one of my favorite cities, New Orleans, where okra and gumbo are staples of the cuisine served there.

My recipe calls for fresh okra because the freshness can't be duplicated. When I purchase the vegetables, I look for firm, brightly colored pods under four inches long because I find the longer pods too tough and fibrous for my taste. Also available canned or frozen, okra gives off a rather viscous substance when cooked that thickens any liquid in which it is heated.

Served with plain white or brown rice and crusty French, Italian, or country bread, this dish would be Creole-perfect.

> 2   teaspoons vegetable oil
> 1   medium green bell pepper, sliced
> 2   cups sliced fresh okra
> 1½ cups fresh corn kernels, or 10-ounce package
>   frozen whole kernel corn
> 2   large ripe tomatoes, roughly chopped, with juice
> 1   teaspoon hot pepper sauce or to taste
>   Salt to taste

1. Heat oil in a nonstick skillet. Add pepper and okra, and cook over medium heat, stirring frequently, for 5 minutes.

2. Add corn, tomatoes, and hot pepper sauce. Reduce heat to low, cover, and simmer gently for about 5 minutes or until vegetables are tender and ingredients are hot. Add a small amount of water, if necessary, to prevent scorching.

3. Remove from heat, taste and adjust seasoning before serving.

SERVES 4 V

PER SERVING: 120 CALORIES; 3.8 GRAMS PROTEIN; 22.5 GRAMS CARBOHYDRATES; 3.1 GRAMS FAT; 0 MILLIGRAMS CHOLESTEROL; 35 MILLIGRAMS SODIUM (WITHOUT SALTING).

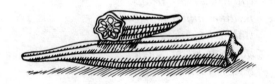

♦ ♦ ♦ ♦ ♦
BLACK RICE AND BEANS JALAPEÑO
▶ ▶

Here, a "quick-cook" method replaces the usual eight-hour soaking of dried beans: beans are boiled briefly, allowed to stand for one hour, then simmered until tender. As with all cooking techniques for dried beans, the actual cooking time will vary depending on the age and condition of the beans.

While cooking, the beans' black skin casts its dye on the rice, giving this dish a rich, ebony-colored finish. For counterpoint, serve with a watercress, arugula, or romaine lettuce salad, a bowl of your favorite salsa, and a covered basket filled with hot corn or wheat tortillas.

1	cup dried black beans
1	medium onion, sliced
1	stalk celery, sliced
1	medium carrot, sliced
1	medium tomato, quartered
1	clove garlic
1	small jalapeño pepper, cored, seeded, and minced (*wear gloves*)
	Salt and freshly ground pepper to taste
1	cup rice
1½	cups water
2	teaspoons chopped fresh basil or cilantro

1. Place beans in a large saucepan. Add enough water to cover and bring to a boil. Cover and cook for 10 minutes. Remove from heat and allow to stand, partially covered, for

1 hour. Add more hot water, if necessary, to keep beans covered.

2. Drain beans and return to saucepan. Add onion, celery, carrots, tomato, garlic, jalapeño pepper, and water to cover.

3. Cover pan, and cook until beans are tender, about 1 to 1½ hours, depending on age of beans. Add water as necessary. Beans should always be covered by liquid while cooking. Season to taste.

4. Combine rice and 1½ cups water in another saucepan. Cover and cook over low heat for about 20 minutes or until rice is tender and liquid is absorbed.

5. Spoon rice into a shallow serving bowl and top with beans and its cooking liquid. Sprinkle with basil or cilantro before serving.

SERVES 4 V
PER SERVING: 360 CALORIES; 14.6 GRAMS PROTEIN; 73.4 GRAMS CARBOHYDRATES; 1.3 GRAMS FAT; 0 MILLIGRAMS CHOLESTEROL; 85 MILLIGRAMS SODIUM (WITHOUT SALTING).

SIDE DISHES

♦ ♦ ♦ ♦ ♦

WINE-BRAISED ARTICHOKES

▶ ▶

Fragrant and flavorful, this combination is one I have prepared with great success over the years. I find it to be the perfect companion for my most elegant main courses.

6–8	*young, firm artichokes*
2	*medium lemons*
1	*tablespoon olive oil*
1	*cup chopped white onion*
2	*medium carrots, scraped and diced*
2	*large cloves garlic, coarsely chopped*
¾	*cup Chablis or other mildly fruity white wine*
1	*tablespoon chopped fresh thyme or 1 teaspoon dried*
1	*small bay leaf*
	Salt and freshly ground pepper to taste

1. Squeeze the juice of 1 lemon into a bowl of cold water large enough to hold all of the artichokes.

2. Remove all tough outer leaves from artichokes and trim stem to a half inch. Snip off tips of remaining leaves, cut artichokes in quarters lengthwise, and remove any fuzzy chokes. As each artichoke is prepared, plunge it into the lemon water to keep it from discoloring.

3. When all artichokes are prepared, heat the oil in a large, deep, nonstick skillet. Add onion and carrots and sauté over medium-low heat until softened but not brown. Stir in garlic and cook for 2 minutes.

4. Drain artichokes and add to the skillet, stirring to coat them with the onion and carrots.

5. Add wine and juice from remaining lemon. Bring to a boil, then reduce heat to low and stir in thyme, bay leaf, and salt and pepper. Simmer gently for 5 minutes, stirring frequently. Reduce heat, cover, and simmer gently, shaking skillet occasionally, for about 30 minutes or until artichokes are tender and liquid is reduced. Sprinkle with salt and pepper and serve with other vegetables from the skillet.

SERVES 6 V

PER SERVING: 110 CALORIES; 4.6 GRAMS PROTEIN; 19.3 GRAMS CARBOHYDRATES; 2.8 GRAMS FAT; 0 MILLIGRAMS CHOLESTEROL; 125 MILLIGRAMS SODIUM (WITHOUT SALTING).

BEANS AND CHARD
WITH SHALLOT SAUCE

▶▶▶▶▶▶▶▶▶▶▶▶▶▶▶▶▶▶▶▶▶▶▶▶▶

Also referred to as "Swiss chard," this member of the beet family is usually found during the summer and has crinkly green leaves that can be prepared like spinach. Chard is a good source of vitamins A and C, as well as iron. If unavailable, use spinach leaves or escarole.

1	pound Swiss chard, trimmed of tough stems, well rinsed, and torn into large pieces
1	tablespoon olive oil
3	large shallots, finely chopped
2	large cloves garlic, chopped, or to taste
¼	cup Vegetable Stock (page 19) or canned low sodium broth
1	bay leaf
1	medium tomato, peeled, seeded, and finely chopped
	Salt and freshly ground pepper to taste
2	cups cooked white kidney beans, or canned (no-salt-added or well-rinsed), drained

1. In a large pot, steam chard in the water clinging to the leaves until wilted. Set aside.

2. Heat oil in a deep, nonstick skillet. Add shallots and cook over medium heat, stirring occasionally, for about 5 minutes or until translucent. Add garlic and continue to cook until shallots show flecks of gold.

3. Add stock, bay leaf, and tomato to skillet. Bring to a

boil, reduce heat to medium-low, and cook for 5 minutes. Taste and add salt and pepper.

4. Add beans to skillet and heat through. Spoon wilted chard on top, reduce heat to very low, cover skillet and simmer gently for 5 minutes.

5. To serve, remove and discard bay leaf, divide chard and beans among heated plates and pour equal portions of sauce from skillet over servings.

SERVES 4 V

PER SERVING: 190 CALORIES; 10.3 GRAMS PROTEIN; 29.9 GRAMS CARBOHYDRATES; 4.1 GRAMS FAT; 0 MILLIGRAMS CHOLESTEROL; 235 MILLIGRAMS SODIUM (WITHOUT SALTING).

♦ ♦ ♦ ♦ ♦

CARROT AND
SWEET POTATO PURÉE

▶ ▶

Here is a guilt-free version of one of my most cherished favorites. Gone is the high-octane butter and heavy cream. Just the sweet and creamy taste remain. I particularly adore it around Thanksgiving time.

3	*medium carrots, peeled and diced*
2	*medium sweet potatoes, peeled and diced*
¼	*cup orange juice*
1	*tablespoon margarine*
1	*teaspoon nutmeg or to taste*
	Salt and freshly ground pepper to taste
2	*teaspoons brown sugar*

1. In a large pot, cover carrots and sweet potatoes with water and bring to a boil. Lower heat, cover, and simmer gently for about 20 minutes or until tender.

2. Meanwhile, preheat oven to 375° F.

3. When vegetables are tender, drain well and transfer to a mixing bowl. Add juice, margarine, nutmeg, salt and pepper to carrots-sweet potatoes and mash until very well blended or transfer to a food processor and purée.

4. Spoon mixture into an ovenproof serving dish and sprinkle top with sugar. Bake for 15 minutes. Serve immediately.

SERVES 4 V

PER SERVING: 140 CALORIES; 1.8 GRAMS PROTEIN; 26.2 GRAMS CARBOHYDRATES; 3.3 GRAMS FAT; 0 MILLIGRAMS CHOLESTEROL; 55 MILLIGRAMS SODIUM (WITHOUT SALTING).

◆ ◆ ◆ ◆ ◆

BRAISED CELERY

▶ ▶

W hat? No onions? Not a garlic clove in sight? Can it be true? Can it be good? You bet it's good! The pungent sage imparts its musty taste and aroma to the braised celery, producing an interesting partner for a boldly sauced entrée.

1   large bunch celery
2   cups Vegetable Stock (page 19) or canned low
     sodium broth
½   teaspoon dried crumbled sage or to_taste
     Salt and freshly ground pepper to taste

1. Trim tops and root ends of celery, separate into stalks and rinse well. Cut each stalk into 2 pieces and place in one layer in a deep, large skillet.

2. Pour stock over celery, and sprinkle with sage and salt and pepper to taste. Cover and cook over medium-low heat for about 45 minutes or until celery is tender. Check occasionally to be sure liquid has not evaporated; add a little more stock or water, if necessary. Taste, adjust seasonings accordingly, and transfer to a serving dish. Serve hot.

SERVES 4 V
PER SERVING: 30 CALORIES; 1.0 GRAMS PROTEIN; 6.2 GRAMS CARBOHYDRATES; .4 GRAMS FAT; 0 MILLIGRAMS CHOLESTEROL; 120 MILLIGRAMS SODIUM (WITHOUT SALTING).

◆ ◆ ◆ ◆ ◆

SPICED CORN

▶▶▶▶▶▶▶▶▶▶▶▶▶▶▶▶▶▶▶▶▶▶▶▶

$\mathbb{S}$callions, mustard, and allspice are added to corn, then thickened with a bit of flour dissolved in water. No fat, no fuss, just an attractive-looking and good-tasting side dish that everyone seems to enjoy.

2½	cups corn kernels, fresh or frozen and thawed
5–6	scallions, white and tender greens, coarsely chopped
1	cup plus 2 tablespoons water
2	teaspoons dry mustard
½	teaspoon allspice
	Salt and freshly ground pepper to taste
	Dash hot pepper sauce or to taste (optional)
1	tablespoon fine flour

1. Combine corn and scallions in a saucepan. Add 1 cup water and bring to a boil. Lower heat and simmer gently, stirring occasionally, for 10 minutes.

2. Add mustard, allspice, salt and pepper, and hot pepper sauce to taste. Stir over low heat until thoroughly blended.

3. Blend flour with remaining 2 tablespoons water and stir into corn mixture. Stir over medium heat until thickened. Serve hot.

SERVES 4 V

PER SERVING: 100 CALORIES; 3.4 GRAMS PROTEIN; 20.0 GRAMS CARBOHYDRATES; .5 GRAMS FAT; 0 MILLIGRAMS CHOLESTEROL; 20 MILLIGRAMS SODIUM (WITHOUT SALTING).

◆◆◆◆◆

MUSHROOMS HUNGARIAN

▶▶▶▶▶▶▶▶▶▶▶▶▶▶▶▶▶▶▶▶▶

The savvy Hungarians have long used paprika as a mainstay flavoring rather than just a garnish. Its taste can range from the familiar mild or sweet variety to the hot and pungent; its color will vary from bright orange-red to a deep blood red. Hungarian paprika, both hot and mild, are considered by many to be superior to others.

Serve this dish with your favorite broad noodle recipes.

> 2 tablespoons Vegetable Stock (page 19) or canned low sodium broth
> 1 clove garlic, crushed
> ¾ pound mushrooms, wiped clean and thinly sliced
> ¼ teaspoon sweet paprika
> ⅛ teaspoon hot paprika
> ½ cup plain low fat yogurt
> Salt to taste

1. Heat stock in a saucepan. Add garlic and cook, stirring, for 30 seconds. Add mushrooms and sweet and hot paprika to saucepan and stir to combine. Cover and cook over low heat for 10 to 15 minutes or until mushrooms are tender.

2. Add yogurt and continue cooking until sauce is heated through; do not allow to boil. Season with salt if desired, and serve.

SERVES 4

PER SERVING: 45 CALORIES; 3.3 GRAMS PROTEIN; 6.4 GRAMS CARBOHYDRATES; .8 GRAMS FAT; 1.8 MILLIGRAMS CHOLESTEROL; 25 MILLIGRAMS SODIUM (WITHOUT SALTING).

◆◆◆◆◆
SAVORY MUSHROOM GRATIN
▶▶▶▶▶▶▶▶▶▶▶▶▶▶▶▶▶▶▶▶▶▶

Very French. This gorgeous gratin is the perfect foil for polenta and a garlicky salad of mixed greens. Or try it at lunch with a salad and a crisp, dry white wine.

½ cup fine bread crumbs, made from 1 slice dried
    whole wheat bread
1 tablespoon minced fresh parsley
½ teaspoon each crushed fresh thyme and rosemary
    or ¼ teaspoon dried (optional)
½ ounce Gruyère cheese, finely shredded
2 teaspoons olive oil
5 cups thickly sliced white mushrooms
1 clove garlic, minced
½ cup dry white wine
    Salt and freshly ground pepper to taste
2 tablespoons all-purpose flour
¾ cup evaporated skim milk

1. Preheat oven to 375° F.

2. In a small bowl, combine bread crumbs, parsley, thyme, rosemary, and Gruyère and set aside.

3. Heat oil in a large, nonstick skillet. Add mushrooms and garlic and cook, stirring often, for 5 minutes, or until mushrooms have given up their liquid. Stir in wine and cook until liquid has nearly evaporated. Taste and add salt and pepper, if desired.

4. Transfer ingredients in skillet to a baking dish or four individual gratin dishes.

5. Whisk together flour and milk and pour over mushroom mixture. Top with bread crumb mixture.

6. Place baking dish on a cookie sheet and bake in center of oven for 20 minutes. Reset oven to broil and broil gratin until crumbs are lightly toasted. Serve hot.

SERVES 4

PER SERVING: 135 CALORIES; 7.4 GRAMS PROTEIN; 16.7 GRAMS CARBOHYDRATES; 4.3 GRAMS FAT; 4.2 MILLIGRAMS CHOLESTEROL; 110 MILLIGRAMS SODIUM (WITHOUT SALTING).

GARLICKY LENTILS

Lentils make this dish nutritional, the spices make it sensational. I prepare this recipe frequently, and no matter what entrée I feature it with I always include a basket of piping-hot pita as well as a refreshing plate of diced cucumbers, tomatoes, and onion disks.

1½	cups lentils, picked over and rinsed
3	cups water
1	bay leaf
1	medium carrot, diced
3	teaspoons olive oil
1	medium onion, finely chopped
4	cloves garlic, chopped
½	teaspoon fennel seeds
⅛	teaspoon cayenne pepper, or to taste
2	tablespoons chopped fresh parsley
1	tablespoon tarragon vinegar or red wine vinegar
	Salt and freshly ground pepper to taste

1. Combine lentils, water, and bay leaf in a large saucepan and cook, stirring occasionally, for 20 minutes. Add carrot and cook for an additional 20 minutes, or until lentils are tender. Stir occasionally and add additional water if needed.

2. When lentils are nearly cooked, heat 2 teaspoons oil in a deep, nonstick skillet and sauté onion until soft and golden in spots. Add garlic, fennel seeds, and cayenne and cook until garlic is pale golden. Stir in parsley.

3. Drain lentils and carrot, discarding any excess cooking water, and add to skillet along with vinegar and remaining teaspoon oil. Cook, stirring gently, for 3 minutes or until flavors are blended and lentils are heated through. Taste and adjust seasonings, if necessary.

SERVES 4 V

PER SERVING: 300 CALORIES; 20.8 GRAMS PROTEIN; 46.2 GRAMS CARBOHYDRATES; 4.5 GRAMS FAT; 0 MILLIGRAMS CHOLESTEROL; 20 MILLIGRAMS SODIUM (WITHOUT SALTING).

SCALLOPED POTATOES
AND PARSNIPS

▶ ▶

Whenever I "slip into something comfortable," inevitably I turn to this homey, satisfying comfort food that contains thin layered slices of potatoes, parsnips, and onion baked in a white sauce.

In this version, I make use of cooking spray and skim milk to reduce the fat content to a bare minimum without losing any flavor.

> Vegetable oil cooking spray
> 3 medium potatoes, peeled and cut into ¼-inch slices
> 2 small parsnips, peeled and cut into ¼-inch slices
> 1 large Spanish onion, sliced into thin rings
> Salt and freshly ground pepper to taste
> 2 tablespoons fine flour
> 1¼ cups evaporated skim milk
> ½ cup water

1. Preheat oven to 375° F.

2. Coat a shallow baking dish, pie plate, or ovenproof casserole with cooking spray. Cover bottom with a layer of potatoes, overlapping them slightly; spread some of the parsnip over them and cover parsnips with onion rings. Repeat another layer of potatoes, parsnips, and onions, then cover with a layer of potatoes.

3. Combine salt and pepper to taste with flour, milk, and water. Stir until smoothly blended and pour mixture over vegetable slices. Coat top lightly with vegetable oil

spray. Cover loosely with foil and bake in preheated oven for 30 minutes.

4. Remove foil and bake for an additional 15 to 20 minutes, or until vegetables are tender and top is lightly browned.

SERVES 4

PER SERVING: 205 CALORIES; 8.9 GRAMS PROTEIN; 40.1 GRAMS CARBOHYDRATES; 1.1 GRAMS FAT; .6 MILLIGRAMS CHOLESTEROL; 110 MILLIGRAMS SODIUM (WITHOUT SALTING).

SPINACH WITH
RAISINS AND PINE NUTS

▶ ▶

One of the cherished dishes of the Sephardic cuisine as well as the so-called "Jewish Ghetto" of Rome, this combination is quite universal in appeal. Splendid with both savory and sweet entrées.

¼	cup raisins
2	tablespoons pine nuts
2	teaspoons olive oil
	Vegetable oil cooking spray
¼	cup Vegetable Stock (page 19) or canned low sodium broth
2	pounds fresh spinach, well rinsed, drained, and trimmed of tough stems
1	teaspoon freshly grated orange rind
	Salt and freshly ground pepper to taste

1. In a small bowl, cover raisins with hot water and set aside.

2. Warm a nonstick skillet over low heat and sprinkle in pine nuts. Cook, shaking pan, until nuts are lightly golden. Remove from heat, transfer nuts to a bowl, and set aside.

3. Coat the skillet lightly with cooking spray, add the oil and warm over medium heat. Add the broth and spinach, cover skillet and cook spinach until wilted.

4. Drain raisins and add to skillet, along with pine nuts and orange rind. Taste and add salt and pepper, if desired. Serve hot.

SERVES 4 V

PER SERVING: 115 CALORIES; 6.1 GRAMS PROTEIN; 14.0 GRAMS CARBOHYDRATES; 5.9 GRAMS FAT; 0 MILLIGRAMS CHOLESTEROL; 135 MILLIGRAMS SODIUM (WITHOUT SALTING).

◆ ◆ ◆ ◆ ◆

RICE AND PEAS
PARMESAN

▶ ▶

This recipe is my slimmed-down version of the classic
Venetian favorite *risi e pisi*, a blend of Arborio rice and
green peas, often made with prosciutto, butter, stock, and/
or cream.

2	*teaspoons vegetable oil*
1	*small onion, finely chopped*
1	*cup rice*
1½	*cups Vegetable Stock (page 19) or canned low sodium broth*
½	*cup green peas, fresh or frozen and thawed*
½	*tablespoon chopped fresh parsley*
2	*tablespoons grated low fat Parmesan cheese*
	Salt and freshly ground pepper to taste

1. Heat oil in a saucepan and add onion. Cook over
medium-high heat, stirring, for 1 minute.

2. Add rice and stock to saucepan. Cover and cook over
low heat for 15 minutes. Add peas and more stock if needed,
and cook an additional 5 minutes or until rice is tender but
not mushy.

3. Remove from heat, stir in parsley and cheese, and
season to taste before serving.

SERVES 4

PER SERVING: 225 CALORIES; 6.0 GRAMS PROTEIN; 43.0
GRAMS CARBOHYDRATES; 3.3 GRAMS FAT; 1.4 MILLIGRAMS
CHOLESTEROL; 65 MILLIGRAMS SODIUM (WITHOUT SALTING).

◆ ◆ ◆ ◆ ◆

ORANGE-BAKED
ACORN SQUASH

▶ ▶

The ginger, cinnamon, and cardamom turns simple squash into a Bombay treat.

2	*small acorn squash*
¾	*teaspoon ground ginger*
½	*teaspoon ground cinnamon*
½	*teaspoon ground cardamom*
4	*tablespoons orange juice, approximate*

1. Preheat oven to 375° F.

2. Cut each squash in half and remove seeds and fibers. Place squash halves, cut side up, in a shallow baking pan and sprinkle evenly with ginger, cinnamon, and cardamom. Add 1 tablespoon orange juice to the cavity of each squash half. Cover with foil and bake for about 30 minutes or until squash is almost tender.

3. Uncover and continue baking, adding a little more orange juice if squash appears dry, for 10 minutes or until squash is browned and tender. Serve hot.

SERVES 4 V

PER SERVING: 75 CALORIES; 1.5 GRAMS PROTEIN; 19.0 GRAMS CARBOHYDRATES; 0 GRAMS FAT; 0 MILLIGRAMS CHOLESTEROL; 10 MILLIGRAMS SODIUM (WITHOUT SALTING).

◆ ◆ ◆ ◆ ◆

SUMMER SQUASH
WITH DILL

▶▶▶▶▶▶▶▶▶▶▶▶▶▶▶▶▶▶▶▶▶▶▶

Here, zucchini and/or yellow squash is lightly flavored, then browned in a bit of oil and sprinkled with dill to add zest.

4   small zucchini and/or yellow squash, about 4
    inches long
    Salt and freshly ground pepper to taste
2   tablespoons flour
2   teaspoons vegetable oil
3   tablespoons fresh chopped dill weed or 1½
    tablespoon dried

1. Trim ends from squash and cut crosswise into ½-inch slices. Combine salt and pepper with flour in plastic bag. Add squash and shake to coat with flour mixture.

2. Heat oil in a large, nonstick skillet and add squash. Cook over medium heat, turning slices to brown evenly, for 8 minutes. Transfer to a serving dish and sprinkle with dill before serving.

SERVES 4 V
PER SERVING: 55 CALORIES; 1.8 GRAMS PROTEIN; 6.5 GRAMS CARBOHYDRATES; 2.5 GRAMS FAT; 0 MILLIGRAMS CHOLESTEROL; 5 MILLIGRAMS SODIUM (WITHOUT SALTING).

◆ ◆ ◆ ◆ ◆

STIR-FRIED VEGETABLES
WITH NECTARINES

▶ ▶

This dish is a nifty supporting player for your favorite Oriental rice or noodle preparation. If nectarines are unavailable, use peaches, plums, jicamas, or apples instead.

2	teaspoons vegetable oil
½	pound snowpeas, trimmed
½	pound thinly sliced mushrooms
1	small onion, thinly sliced
1	clove garlic, pressed
1	cup fresh bean sprouts
2	teaspoons low sodium soy sauce
2	medium nectarines, cut into bite-size chunks

1. Heat oil in a large, nonstick skillet. Add snowpeas, mushrooms, onion, garlic, bean sprouts, and soy sauce.

2. Cook over medium heat, stirring, for about 10 minutes or until vegetables are just tender. Add nectarine chunks and heat through, stirring gently. Serve hot.

SERVES 4 V

PER SERVING: 110 CALORIES; 4.5 GRAMS PROTEIN; 18.0 GRAMS CARBOHYDRATES; 3.0 GRAMS FAT; 0 MILLIGRAMS CHOLESTEROL; 105 MILLIGRAMS SODIUM (WITHOUT SALTING).

REFRIED PINTO BEANS

▶ ▶

How versatile can you get? Very! Try it as a side dish, as a main dish over hot rice, or wrapped in tortillas, diluted for a soup, even chilled for a spread. I think you'll find this recipe invaluable.

1¼	cups pinto beans, picked over, soaked overnight, rinsed and drained
5	cups water
1	cup dry red wine
1	tablespoon vegetable oil
1	large onion, chopped
1	medium green or red bell pepper, trimmed and diced
1	small stalk celery, diced
2	cups chopped fresh or canned (no-salt-added) tomatoes, with juice
½	cup canned no-salt-added tomato sauce
¼	cup minced fresh cilantro or parsley
1	teaspoon chili powder
½	teaspoon cumin
½	teaspoon dry mustard
	Salt and freshly ground pepper to taste
	Hot pepper flakes to taste (optional)

1. Place beans in a saucepan and add water and wine. Bring to a boil, then lower heat and simmer gently for about 2 hours, or until beans are tender. Drain and reserve some of the cooking liquid, if any. Let cool slightly.

2. When beans are almost done, heat oil in a large, nonstick skillet. Add onion, pepper, and celery and cook over medium heat, stirring often, for 5 minutes. Stir in tomatoes, tomato sauce, cilantro, and seasonings, and simmer gently for 5 minutes.

3. Put cooled beans into a food processor and process very briefly. Beans should be coarsely puréed and have a slightly runny consistency, so add a little reserved cooking liquid or additional water or stock, if needed.

4. Add beans to skillet with vegetables and cook over medium heat, stirring often, until mixture is thickened and reduced to about 4 cups.

SERVES 6 V
PER SERVING: 290 CALORIES; 14.5 GRAMS PROTEIN; 49.2 GRAMS CARBOHYDRATES; 4.5 GRAMS FAT; 0 MILLIGRAMS CHOLESTEROL; 45 MILLIGRAMS SODIUM (WITHOUT SALTING).

◆◆◆◆◆

GINGERED TOMATOES

▶▶▶▶▶▶▶▶▶▶▶▶▶▶▶▶▶▶▶▶▶▶▶▶▶

A quick, easy, and delicious side dish—especially good with couscous, polenta, or other grain entrée.

4   large ripe tomatoes, cut crosswise into thick slices
1   tablespoon freshly grated ginger
1½ tablespoons fresh lime juice
2   scallions, with tops, chopped
    Salt and freshly ground pepper to taste

1. Arrange tomatoes on a serving platter or individual dishes.

2. Combine ginger with lime juice and spoon mixture evenly over tomatoes. Sprinkle with scallions and seasonings, and serve at room temperature.

SERVES 4 V

PER SERVING: 50 CALORIES; 1.9 GRAMS PROTEIN; 11.1 GRAMS CARBOHYDRATES; .7 GRAMS FAT; 0 MILLIGRAMS CHOLESTEROL; 20 MILLIGRAMS SODIUM (WITHOUT SALTING).

DESSERTS

APPLE BREAD PUDDING

▶▶▶▶▶▶▶▶▶▶▶▶▶▶▶▶▶▶▶▶▶▶▶▶▶

Kid stuff? Of course it is! And yet this pudding is unde-
niably sophisticated, what with the melding of seasonings
that include a spicy-sweet nip of cardamom. Should you
desire a topping, a dollop of nonfat plain yogurt flavored
with dark rum makes an excellent one.

Fresh raspberries (about 2 cups) can be successfully
substituted for the apples.

2½	cups large cubes of day-old French bread
2	Granny Smith or other tart apples, peeled, cored, and cubed
¼	cup golden seedless raisins
1	teaspoon vanilla extract
⅛	teaspoon ground nutmeg
⅛	teaspoon ground cinnamon
⅛	teaspoon ground cardamom
	Egg substitute equal to 3 eggs or 1 large egg and 2 egg whites
2	tablespoons white sugar
2	tablespoons brown sugar
1	tablespoon unbleached all-purpose flour
2	cups low fat (2%) milk

1. Preheat oven to 350° F.

2. Arrange half of the bread cubes in the bottom of a
1½-quart baking dish. Add half of the apple cubes and raisins
and sprinkle with the spices. Cover with remaining bread
cubes, then top with remaining apples and raisins.

3. Beat egg substitute or eggs with sugars.

4. Whisk flour into milk and add to egg blend. Pour egg-milk mixture over ingredients in baking dish.

5. Place baking dish in a larger pan and add hot water to come halfway up the side of the baking dish. Bake in preheated oven for 1 hour or until set.

SERVES 6

PER SERVING: 200 CALORIES; 7.8 GRAMS PROTEIN; 36.5 GRAMS CARBOHYDRATES; 2.0 GRAMS FAT; 5 MILLIGRAMS CHOLESTEROL; 215 MILLIGRAMS SODIUM.

LIGHT LINZERTORTE

▶ ▶

Linz, Austria, is the birthplace of this justifiably famous torte. Classically, it is made with a very buttery crust that is usually smeared with raspberry jam then capped with a latticed crust. My version lowers the fat content of the original but not its elegant, rich flavor.

For a twist on the traditional raspberry filling, substitute peach, apricot, or a mixture of fruits.

1¼	ounces hazelnuts
⅔	cup unbleached all-purpose flour
¼	cup rolled oats
¼	teaspoon baking soda
¼	teaspoon salt
	Pinch ground cloves
	Pinch grated nutmeg
	Pinch finely ground black pepper
2½	tablespoons chilled margarine, cut in small pieces
	Egg substitute equal to 2 eggs or 1 large egg and 1 egg white
	Vegetable oil cooking spray
1½	cups raspberry low sugar preserves or fruit spread
2	teaspoons grated lemon rind

1. Put hazelnuts in a food processor and process with on/off motions until finely ground. Transfer nuts to a small bowl; do not clean food processor bowl.

2. Combine flour, oats, baking soda, salt, and spices in food processor and process briefly, just to blend. Add

margarine a piece at a time and process until mixture has a coarse consistency. Add egg substitute or beaten egg and ground nuts and process just until mixture holds together.

3. Form dough into a ball, wrap in plastic and refrigerate for 30 minutes.

4. On a large piece of wax paper lightly dusted with flour, roll out two-thirds of the dough into a 9-inch-diameter circle. Press dough circle into an 8-inch nonstick fluted tart pan so that dough comes about 1 inch up the sides. Cover and refrigerate for 30 minutes. (Crust can be made ahead and refrigerated, well covered, for 24 hours.)

5. Preheat oven to 375° F.

6. Combine fruit spread and lemon rind. Add to chilled crust and spread evenly.

7. Roll out remaining dough and either cut in strips to form a lattice top or cut out decorative shapes (hearts, flowers, diamonds, etc.) and lay on top of fruit. Bake for 30 minutes. Let cool before serving.

SERVES 6

PER SERVING: 285 CALORIES; 4.6 GRAMS PROTEIN; 38.6 GRAMS CARBOHYDRATES; 14.8 GRAMS FAT; 0 MILLIGRAMS CHOLESTEROL; 185 MILLIGRAMS SODIUM.

CHOCOLATE YOGURT MENINGUE PIE

▶▶▶▶▶▶▶▶▶▶▶▶▶▶▶▶▶▶▶▶▶▶▶▶▶

A variation on the meringue pie theme, here the meringue is spooned into the pan and baked for an hour. After cooling, it then becomes the crust, not the topping. The cooled crust is then filled with nonfat frozen chocolate yogurt and garnished with shaved chocolate.

	Vegetable oil cooking spray
3	egg whites, at room temperature
1/8	teaspoon cream of tartar
1/3	cup sugar
1/8	teaspoon salt
1	teaspoon vanilla or almond extract
2	cups (1 pint) fat-free chocolate frozen yogurt, softened
1/2	ounce semisweet chocolate, shaved

1. Preheat oven to 250° F. Lightly coat a 9-inch pie pan with cooking spray and set aside.

2. Beat egg whites until frothy, then add cream of tartar and salt. Continue to beat, adding sugar gradually, until stiff, glossy peaks form. Beat in vanilla or almond extract.

3. Spoon meringue into prepared pie pan. Using the back of a spoon, spread mixture to cover bottom and sides, but not the rim of pan, making sides slightly thicker than bottom and higher than rim of pan.

4. Bake for 1 hour or until meringue is firm, then turn

oven off and let crust dry without opening oven door. Do not remove until oven is cool.

5. Fill cooled crust with softened frozen yogurt and garnish top with chocolate shavings. Refreeze before serving, if necessary, and dip knife in warm water to facilitate slicing pie.

SERVES 6

PER SERVING: 140 CALORIES; 3.9 GRAMS PROTEIN; 28.7 GRAMS CARBOHYDRATES; 1.4 GRAMS FAT; 0 MILLIGRAMS CHOLESTEROL; 110 MILLIGRAMS SODIUM.

◆◆◆◆◆

STRAWBERRY-APPLE TART

▶▶▶▶▶▶▶▶▶▶▶▶▶▶▶▶▶▶▶▶▶▶▶▶

The sweetness of the strawberries and sugar makes a wonderful contrast to the tartness of the Granny Smith apples. The pie crust recipe makes a crispy, light crust well suited for a variety of fillings.

BASIC PIE CRUST
  1   cup plus 2 tablespoons unbleached all-purpose
       flour
  1   teaspoon sugar
  3   tablespoons chilled margarine, cut into 6 pieces
  2   tablespoons ice water, approximately
  ⅛   teaspoon salt (optional)

FILLING
  3   Granny Smith or other tart apples, peeled, cored,
       and sliced
  ⅓   cup apple juice
  2   tablespoons fresh lemon juice
  2   tablespoons unbleached all-purpose flour
  2   cups sliced fresh strawberries
  3   tablespoons sugar

1. Combine flour and sugar, if desired, in a food processor. With machine on, add margarine a piece at a time and process until mixture has a coarse consistency. Gradually add water, and continue processing until mixture forms a ball; add a little more ice water, if necessary. Remove dough

from processor, wrap in foil, and chill in refrigerator for 30 minutes.

2. Preheat oven to 350° F.

3. Roll out chilled dough on a floured surface and fit into a 9-inch nonstick pie plate or tart pan. Prick bottom of dough, and bake for 10 minutes. Remove crust, and let cool to room temperature. Do not turn off oven.

4. Toss apples with apple and lemon juices and flour. Add strawberries and toss gently to combine. Spoon mixture into pie crust and sprinkle top with sugar.

5. Place pie on baking sheet in center rack of oven. Bake for 20 to 30 minutes, or until apples are tender and lightly browned. Allow to cool before serving.

SERVES 6 V

PER SERVING: 240 CALORIES; 3.2 GRAMS PROTEIN; 43.8 GRAMS CARBOHYDRATES; 6.3 GRAMS FAT; 0 MILLIGRAMS CHOLESTEROL; 100 MILLIGRAMS SODIUM (WITHOUT SALT-ING).

◆ ◆ ◆ ◆ ◆

FRESH FRUIT
ALMOND-CUSTARD TART

▶ ▶

Because evaporated skim and low fat milks are used, this creamy dessert has a small fraction of the fat contained in more traditional custard recipes. The choice of fruits is up to you. If you prefer, substitute (or add) other thinly sliced fresh fruits, including bananas, peaches, nectarines, and plums.

1	Basic Pie Crust (page 183, step 1)
1/4	cup cornstarch
1	cup evaporated skim milk
2	cups low fat (2%) milk
3	tablespoons honey
1/3	cup egg substitute
1	teaspoon almond extract
1/2	cup thinly sliced strawberries
1/2	cup thinly sliced trimmed kiwifruit
1/2	cup fresh blueberries
3	seedless red grapes, cut in half lengthwise

1. Preheat oven to 350° F.

2. Roll out chilled pie crust dough on a floured surface and fit into a fluted 8- or 9-inch tart pan. Prick bottom of dough, and bake in preheated oven for 15 to 20 minutes or until lightly browned. Remove from oven and set aside to cool.

3. To make custard, combine cornstarch and skim milk in a large saucepan and whisk until smooth. Add low fat milk

and honey and whisk over low heat until hot and well blended. Raise heat to medium and cook, stirring constantly, until mixture thickens and just begins to boil. Remove from heat.

4. Put egg substitute in a small mixing bowl and stir in 2 tablespoons of hot custard mixture. Pour egg mixture into custard in saucepan. Add almond extract and stir well to combine all ingredients.

5. Transfer custard to a bowl and let cool to room temperature, stirring several times. Refrigerate until ready to assemble.

6. Before serving, whisk custard smooth and pour or spoon into baked tart crust. Starting from outside rim, cover custard with alternating strawberries, kiwifruit, and blueberries; place grapes so they radiate from center of tart.

SERVES 6

PER SERVING: 285 CALORIES; 9.5 GRAMS PROTEIN; 45.2 GRAMS CARBOHYDRATES; 7.5 GRAMS FAT; 5.3 MILLIGRAMS CHOLESTEROL; 215 MILLIGRAMS SODIUM.

PUMPKIN CHEESECAKE

▶ ▶

Just when you thought there was no place in your healthy lifestyle for cheesecake, along comes this marvelous recipe to the rescue. Just a couple of notes about the ingredients: first, use canned pumpkin—*not* the pumpkin pie filling that is more than three times higher in sugar, and therefore calories, and over 20 times higher in sodium! Also, many producers now make a fat-free ricotta that works just as well as the whole milk or low fat variety for this cake.

CRUST

7	*whole graham crackers (2½ by 5 inches), crushed*
2	*tablespoons sugar*
2	*tablespoons margarine, melted*

FILLING

1	*15-ounce container fat-free ricotta cheese*
	Egg substitute equal to 2 eggs or 1 large egg and 1 egg white
1	*1-pound can pumpkin*
⅓	*cup sugar*
3	*tablespoons brown sugar*
1	*teaspoon ground cinnamon*
½	*teaspoon ground nutmeg*
½	*teaspoon ground ginger*
¼	*teaspoon ground cloves*

1. Preheat oven to 350° F.
2. Combine crust ingredients in a bowl and mash with

fork until thoroughly blended. Transfer to an 8-inch non-stick springform pan (or coat lightly with vegetable oil spray). Pat crust on bottom of pan and about ½ inch up the sides. Set aside.

3. Combine ricotta and egg substitute in food processor and process until smooth. Add remaining ingredients and process until thoroughly blended.

4. Spoon filling into prepared pan and bake for about 1 hour or until center is set and inserted toothpick comes out clean. Remove from oven and let set a few minutes. Run knife carefully around sides to loosen and unmold. Let cool to room temperature before serving. (If serving cool, cover until ready to serve or cake will "sweat.")

SERVES 8

PER SERVING: 180 CALORIES; 9.7 GRAMS PROTEIN; 26.5 GRAMS CARBOHYDRATES; 3.3 GRAMS FAT; 0 MILLIGRAMS CHOLESTEROL; 175 MILLIGRAMS SODIUM.

◆ ◆ ◆ ◆

APRICOT ICE MILK

▶ ▶

Easy to whip together and elegant served in chilled long-stemmed wine goblets, this is a lovely way to cap a good meal.

4	ounces dried apricots
	Boiling water
½	cup sugar
2	cups evaporated skim milk
1	cup low fat (2%) milk
	Egg substitute equal to 2 eggs
1	teaspoon vanilla extract

1. In a bowl, cover apricots with enough boiling water to just cover and let stand until apricots are softened. Drain and finely chop.

2. In a large bowl, combine sugar, milks, egg substitute, and vanilla extract and beat well. Stir in chopped apricots. Pour into freezer container of ice cream maker and process according to manufacturer's instructions. (To freeze without ice cream maker: Pour into a 9- by 13-inch glass baking pan and freeze for about 3 hours or until mixture starts to freeze at edges. Spoon into food processor or blender and process until smooth. Return to freezer and freeze until solid—if not smooth enough, refreeze and reprocess before the final freezing.)

SERVES 6

PER SERVING: 205 CALORIES; 10.0 GRAMS PROTEIN; 39.9 GRAMS CARBOHYDRATES; .9 GRAMS FAT; 3.2 MILLIGRAMS CHOLESTEROL; 150 MILLIGRAMS SODIUM.

◆ ◆ ◆ ◆ ◆

LEMON-CRANBERRY GRANITA

▶▶▶▶▶▶▶▶▶▶▶▶▶▶▶▶▶▶▶▶▶▶▶▶▶

A granita is a popular Italian dessert; a flavored ice made of fine-grained frozen crystals flavored with a fruit syrup or strong coffee. A granita isn't creamy like ice cream or milk or smooth like a sorbet. It's a light, icy dessert, reminiscent of the ices we used to buy on the street as kids—but more elegant.

2 cups water
¼ cup minced fresh cranberries
1 cup cranberry juice
½ cup sugar
1 tablespoon grated fresh lemon peel
½ cup fresh lemon juice
Dash of salt

1. Combine water, cranberries, cranberry juice, and sugar in a saucepan. Bring to a boil, stirring to dissolve sugar. Lower heat to a simmer, and cook for 3 minutes.

2. Add lemon peel, lemon juice, and salt. Remove from heat and stir to combine.

3. Pour into a shallow baking dish, place in freezer, and freeze for 3 hours, or until mixture is icy, stirring every 20 minutes to break up the ice crystals before the granita becomes solid. Allow to soften for about 15 minutes before serving.

SERVES 6 V

PER SERVING: 95 CALORIES; .2 GRAMS PROTEIN; 25.9 GRAMS CARBOHYDRATES; 0 GRAMS FAT; 0 MILLIGRAMS CHOLESTEROL; 25 MILLIGRAMS SODIUM.

POACHED PEARS
WITH RED-CURRANT WINE SAUCE

Truly one of the great desserts of this world, it can also be made with the pears peeled and left whole with the stem intact (but be aware they will take a longer time to become tender).

  1   cup Burgundy or other hearty red table
       wine
  ½   cup apple juice
  3   tablespoons red currant jelly
  ½   teaspoon ground cinnamon (optional)
  ½   teaspoon ground allspice (optional)
  ¼   teaspoon ground cloves (optional)
  4   firm-ripe fresh pears, preferably Bartletts, peeled,
       halved, and cored

1. Combine all ingredients, except pears, in a saucepan. Stir and bring to a boil. Reduce heat to low, add pears, cover, and simmer gently, turning pears often, for about 10 minutes or until pears are tender. Let pears cool slightly in pan with liquid.

2. Transfer pears to a serving dish and spoon over poaching liquid. Serve warm or refrigerate and serve chilled.

SERVES 4 V

PER SERVING: 120 CALORIES; .4 GRAMS PROTEIN; 30.4 GRAMS CARBOHYDRATES; .5 GRAMS FAT; 0 MILLIGRAMS CHOLESTEROL; 5 MILLIGRAMS SODIUM.

◆ ◆ ◆ ◆ ◆

ORANGE-FLAVORED
RICE PUDDING

▶ ▶

I can't think of a more comforting food than rice pudding. My take on this dish is a little unusual inasmuch as I combine long-grained basmati rice and oranges. The flavors complement each other to produce an aromatic, tasty pudding.

2   cups low fat (1%) *milk*
½   cup basmati rice
2   tablespoons sugar
     Egg substitute equal to 1 egg or 1 large egg
1   tablespoon grated orange rind
1   tablespoon orange marmalade
½   teaspoon orange extract

1. Combine milk, rice, and sugar in a saucepan. Heat until mixture comes to a boil. Reduce heat to low, cover, and cook for about 20 minutes or until rice is tender.

2. Spoon half of the rice mixture into the egg substitute or beaten egg. Mix, and pour egg-rice combination into remaining rice. Cook over very low heat for 3 minutes, stirring.

3. Turn off heat. Add orange rind, marmalade, and extract to rice. Mix gently to just combine. Spoon mixture into individual serving dishes and refrigerate for about 3 hours or until rice is set.

SERVES 4

PER SERVING: 130 CALORIES; 5.8 GRAMS PROTEIN; 20.8 GRAMS CARBOHYDRATES; 2.5 GRAMS FAT; 7.5 MILLIGRAMS CHOLESTEROL; 85 MILLIGRAMS SODIUM.

GLAZED CARROT CAKE
WITH RAISINS

Here is a cake that can do triple duty: with or without the glaze, I enjoy it for breakfast, as a nifty between-meal snack and, of course, as a dessert. It's best served warm.

1	cup all-purpose flour
1	teaspoon baking soda
1	teaspoon baking powder
1	teaspoon cardamom
¼	teaspoon salt
⅓	cup vegetable oil
½	cup sugar
1	teaspoon almond extract
	Egg substitute equal to 2 eggs or 1 large egg and 1 egg white
1½	cups grated carrots
¼	cup golden seedless raisins plumped in 1 cup hot water and drained

GLAZE
4	tablespoons apple juice
2	tablespoons confectioners' sugar
1	tablespoon cornstarch

1. Preheat oven to 350° F.

2. Sift together flour, baking soda, baking powder, cardamom, and salt. Reserve.

3. Combine oil, sugar, almond extract, and egg substitute or eggs in a food processor, and process until thoroughly blended.

4. Gradually stir oil-egg mixture into flour mixture. Add grated carrots and drained raisins, and stir until ingredients are thoroughly combined.

5. Pour batter into an 8-inch-square nonstick baking pan, and bake for 30 to 40 minutes or until top is springy to the touch and an inserted toothpick comes out clean. Remove from oven and let cake cool slightly.

6. Prepare glaze while cake cools: Heat 2 tablespoons apple juice in a small saucepan and stir in sugar. Stir over medium heat until mixture starts to simmer. Reduce heat and add cornstarch combined with remaining apple juice. Stir constantly over very low heat for 1 minute or until thickened and heated through. Spoon glaze over warm cake.

MAKES SIXTEEN 2-INCH SQUARES
PER SQUARE: 115 CALORIES; 1.6 GRAMS PROTEIN; 17.2 GRAMS CARBOHYDRATES; 4.7 GRAMS FAT; 0 MILLIGRAMS CHOLESTEROL; 120 MILLIGRAMS SODIUM.

◆ ◆ ◆ ◆ ◆

LIGHT BROWNIE SQUARES

▶ ▶

Do your favorite chocoholic a favor by serving these delicious, light brownies. By using cocoa powder instead of baking chocolate you will reduce the fat but you won't sacrifice the flavor.

　3　tablespoons margarine
　4　tablespoons unsweetened cocoa powder
　　　Egg substitute equal to 1 egg or 1 large egg
　½　teaspoon vanilla extract
　½　cup sugar
　½　cup skim milk
　¾　cup unbleached all-purpose flour
　½　teaspoon baking powder
1–2　tablespoons confectioners' sugar (optional)

1. Preheat oven to 325° F.
2. Melt margarine in a saucepan and stir in cocoa.
3. In a mixing bowl, combine egg substitute or beaten egg, vanilla extract, and sugar. Add margarine-cocoa mixture and stir to blend ingredients. Stir in milk alternately with flour and baking powder, combining well after each addition.
4. Spoon batter into an 8-inch-square nonstick baking pan and bake for 20 minutes or until top is springy to the touch and an inserted toothpick comes out clean. Remove from oven and sprinkle with confectioners' sugar. Cut into 16 squares when cooled.

MAKES SIXTEEN 2-INCH SQUARES

PER SQUARE: 80 CALORIES; 2.0 GRAMS PROTEIN; 12.3 GRAMS CARBOHYDRATES; 2.5 GRAMS FAT; 0 MILLIGRAMS CHOLESTEROL; 40 MILLIGRAMS SODIUM.

INDEX

CORINNE T. NETZER

101

TASTY REASONS FOR HEALTHY EATING

For those watching their intake of
fat, calories, cholesterol, fiber and sodium,
The Corinne T. Netzer
Good Eating Series Cookbooks
offer recipes that are welcome in any kitchen.

___ 50418-X   101 LOW FAT RECIPES • $8.99

___ 50420-1   101 HIGH FIBER RECIPES • $8.99

___ 50416-3   101 LOW CALORIE RECIPES • $8.99

___ 50417-1   101 LOW CHOLESTEROL RECIPES • $8.99

___ 50419-8   101 LOW SODIUM RECIPES • $8.99

___ 50597-6   101 VEGETARIAN RECIPES • $8.99

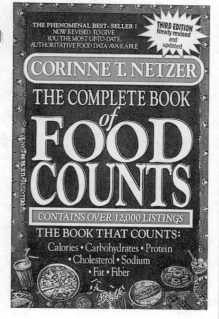